P9-DNO-028

Follow the Blue

Brigid Lowry

Holiday House / New York

In Memory of Pat

Thank you to my kind husband, my wonderful son, my magnificent agent
and my excellent editors. And thanks to Eloise Sweetman, Sophie Greenwood
and Stephanie Johnson, each of whom helped this book along
in their own way.

Acknowledgements
Sam Field for "How to Kickflip."
Zoe Thurner for her advice on magic and the hand basin story.

Copyright © Brigid Lowry, 2001
All Rights Reserved
First published in Australia in 2001 by Allen & Unwin Pty Ltd.,
83 Alexander Street, Crows Nest NSW 2065, Australia.
First publication in the United States by Holiday House, Inc. 2004
Printed in the United States of America
First American Edition
www.holidayhouse.com
1 3 5 7 9 10 8 6 4 2

Library of Congress Cataloging-in-Publication Data

Lowry, Brigid.
Follow the blue / Brigid Lowry.—1st American ed.
p. cm.
Summary: Fifteen-year-old Bec, living with her family in Perth, Australia,
decides to stop being sensible and follow her wilder impulses
during the summer that her parents are away on a long trip
to help her father recover from a breakdown.
ISBN 0-8234-1827-8
[1. Self-perception—Fiction. 2. Conduct of life—Fiction. 3. Interpersonal
relations—Fiction. 4. Brothers and sisters—Fiction.
5. Perth (W.A.)—Fiction. 6. Australia—Fiction.] I. Title.
PZ7.L96725Fo 2004
[Fic]—dc22
2003062550

Cover collage by Verity Prideaux
Cover photograph by Terence Brogue
Text design by Ruth Grüner

blue

The day my father came out of hospital was the day Begonia disappeared. Everything seemed to happen then, that hazy summer, and now it has all melted into one, like an ice-cream that some clumsy kid dropped in the heat. Splat, squelch and dribble. Creamy puddles and sticky goo. It wasn't a bad time, though. I thought it was, for a while, but now, looking back, I can see everything happened just the way it was supposed to.

Stories are mysterious things. Beginning, middle and end, that's what they tell you at school, but life isn't actually neat and tidy like that. It's more like a funny old muddle of weird threads that sometimes has boring bits, and sometimes has tricky bits, and sometimes has just-right bits—like a whole lot of balls of brightly coloured wool thrown in a basket, with stray beginnings and endings and possibilities everywhere, and curly bits and knots and twists. If you pick a colour, like blue, you get a nice straight bit unwinding for a while but then it gets knotted up with green, and before you know it you're all tangled in purple and turquoise, and it takes ages until you get a long smooth piece again.

Let's follow the blue.

My name is Bec. On my birth certificate it says Rebecca Eileen, but I never tell anyone that. If I have a kid I won't name it after a long dead relative, and that's for sure.

I was fifteen last summer, the summer that my parents went away. I'm sixteen now. I'm an ordinary girl. I don't have a nose ring and I don't want one. I don't wear Mambo or Stussy or Poppy lipstick. I don't wear lipstick at all. Vera calls me the sensible one, but I'm not really very sensible. Sometimes I'm dreamy and forgetful. Maybe it is just that I'm more practical than Josh and easier to control than Bing. I am above-average at school. I'm not stunningly brilliant but I don't find school work hard, just a bit boring sometimes. English and Art are my best subjects, and I'm learning French, which I like, except for the masses of vocabulary homework. I play the flute. I ride a bike. My friends are Jaz, Eloise, Julia, Lisa and Katherine. I have brown hair and brown eyes, and when I was little my nickname was Wol, like in *Winnie The Pooh*, because I was a round sweet baby with eyes like raisins, Vera says.

There are five of us in our family. My mother's name is Vera. You might have heard of her because she's a celebrity cook. Her show is called *Vera's Kitchen* and it's on every Friday night at seven-thirty. Maybe you've seen her cookbooks, *Vegetables with Vera* and *Viva Vera!*.

My mother eats and dreams food. She says cooking is a sacred art. Maybe it is, but Vera can be obsessive about it. For example, pasta from a packet is an insult to the human race as far as she is concerned. She makes her own from some kind of special flour and organic eggs, and serves it with butter and wild sage. It takes her ages. I always feel guilty for wolfing it down, which is what I do, because the sage is bitter and the quicker you eat it the less you taste the dodgy flavour.

Vera's hair is wild and curly and as red as plums. 'My power hair', she calls it. She wears heaps of jewellery, silver and gold necklaces and lapis lazuli earrings and garnet rings. 'You're not supposed to mix silver and gold but honey, I think I can get away with this, don't you?' Vera will ask, and my father just smiles. Vera could wear a dress made from a plastic bag, and a pair of gumboots, and Lewis would still think she was gorgeous. He adores her. Clothes don't interest him. My father is more interested in the essence of things.

Lewis is an architect. He specialises in energy efficient buildings and he used to teach at Uni before he had his breakdown. I hate that word. It makes him sound like an old heap of a car with a clapped-out engine or something, but a breakdown, or rather a 'manic episode followed by severe depression', is what the doctor diagnosed.

It was really strange how it happened. Generally my father is a quiet person who thinks things through before he speaks, so the first sign that all was not right with him was when he started talking too much. At dinner he gulped down his food and talked heaps, like he had drunk too much coffee or taken some weird speedy drug. Vera was extremely worried about him but he wouldn't see a doctor. 'I'm fine, baby, just fine,' he said and then started raving on about geodesic domes and fields of light.

My father went up and up like a crazy star and then he fell down into a dark sad place. He wouldn't talk, and he wouldn't eat. He just sat in his squashy green leather armchair and moved his fingers round and round in odd aimless patterns. It was awful. Doctor Patterson put him on to this whizz-bang medication but it didn't seem to help much. Lewis was as grey and quiet as paper. He was nearly not there at all.

Then, one almost ordinary afternoon, my father went out for a walk in the sunshine, and he didn't come home. By evening Vera was in a total panic. We looked and looked for him but Lewis was nowhere to be found. Finally Vera notified the police. Late that night they found my father miles away, in a park, making sculptures from leaves and rocks. Someone had reported him for strange behaviour because he had lit a small fire, and had taken off his brown plaid shirt and hung it in a tree. Vera told us all about it at breakfast. Her face was sad, like a wilted flower, as she sat in her fluffy dressing gown, clutching her latte cup even though the coffee was murky and cold. She said that Lewis was going into hospital for a while so the doctor could try some new treatments that might help him get better.

Every Saturday we went and visited my father, Vera and me

and Josh and Bing. The hospital was an old wooden building surrounded by stately gardens. You could almost pretend it was a posh resort, except for the wonky people wandering around amongst the rose bushes. We took my father gifts of strawberries and cake and glossy architectural magazines. We did our best to be cheerful but we didn't feel cheerful. Despite his new medicine Lewis just sat on the white bench under the oak tree, as sleepy and mournful as an old cocker spaniel. Time moved very slowly on the afternoons we visited my father.

Black is the sorrow colour.

~~~

'When is Dad coming home?' Josh asked every week. My brother is a creature of habit. He always asked the same question at the same place, as we drove home past the fish-and-chip shop near the wharf where the ferries come and go. Each time Vera would answer, 'I just don't know, darling.'

Josh is eleven. He's skinny and dark-haired, and very bright. Josh is deep, like a secret or a puzzle. He knows a lot about everything. He knows the names of every bird and insect, and huge amounts of technical stuff, like he can tell you exactly how a fax operates. Doesn't it seem strange to you that a picture can go down a wire in bits and bytes and magically come out a picture again at the other end? Well, it does to me but not to Josh. He can tell you about it in more technical detail than you would ever expect a boy to know. Josh collects and adores bizarre information of every kind.

'Did you know that in Vietnam there are fifty embalmers employed to find new ways to keep the body of Ho Chi Minh in peak condition for future generations?' Josh usually comes out with something like that just as Vera is trying to get us to hurry up and finish our cashew muesli with soya milk, so she can get us out of the house and get to work. His timing drives my mother bananas. She loves us heaps and is keen to be a perfect mother. She's always reading books about parenting and relationships and stuff but sometimes her patience wears thin, especially when she's in a hurry.

Actually, Josh is not that good with people in general because he likes to explain things in minute detail. 'It's a tiny insect that looks like a hummingbird,' he'll begin, 'which you would think was a tropical species but it's really . . .' Most people's eyes glaze over at around this point. No one seems to have the time for a lot of facts these days. 'Mmm,' they say, but Josh can tell they're not listening properly, and he goes back inside himself like a little crab disappearing into a spotted shell.

~~~

I knew this would happen. I'm all tangled up in a wild wriggle of colours. I begin to tell you about what happened last summer and before I even get to Bing the story is going all over the place, which is rather alarming because Bing is the last person you could ever leave out of anything.

meet the one and only bing

My sister, Bing, is fierce. She is nine years old but she's not like any other nine year old that I ever met. Her real name is Beatrice Rose—after another long dead aunt—but ever since my sister was tiny she's been called Bing. When Vera was pregnant she had a craving and ate cherries by the handful, and Dad joked that the baby would come out all red and round and shiny like a Bing Cherry. Actually when my sister was born she was greyish and crumpled, with yellow fluff on her head, but Bing is a good name for her. Beatrice Rose is the name of a fairy or a pale angelic girl but my sister is tough, all fire and grit. She's hard to describe really. Bing is just Bing, feisty and full-on. Dad sometimes calls her 'Bing Zap Pow'.

Here is something that shows you what my sister is like.

'I want my hair cut, Vera,' Bing announced one morning. I never ask my mother for anything over breakfast, as Vera is not always at her most approachable in the mornings, but Bing is like Josh in that regard. Timing is not their greatest strength.

'Oh, but your hair is absolutely gorgeous. Are you sure, honey?' Vera mumbled as she tucked into her raisin toast.

'Yeah, I want it cut very short,' said Bing firmly. We all stared at Bing and her long, shiny, silvery hair.

'Pity,' said Josh.

'Cut,' said Bing.

'Well, all right then,' said Vera, 'but next week, okay? I've got a huge amount happening right now, chickadee. We have to shoot two shows this week instead of one because of the producer's sinus operation. It's a nightmare, I don't even want to think about it, but next week, okay, Bingy?'

This was a fairly typical response. When Vera thinks she can't get away with saying 'no' she tends to stall things by saying 'later', a trick she no doubt picked up at The Cunning Mother Training School, along with the manoeuvre of offering a 'definite maybe' and other piss-weak devices.

Anyhow, Bing didn't say anything. She just kept ploughing her way through her muesli, carefully picking out all the bits of dried paw-paw to give to Begonia, her guinea pig. Paw-paw, olives, mushrooms . . . all the things Bing doesn't like, Begonia loves. They have a very practical relationship.

I looked over at Josh and winked. She'll forget all about it, right? Josh wrinkled his nose and raised a thoughtful eyebrow, and we all moved on into a day crowded with school and library books and computers and socks and bicycles and eggplants.

That night when Vera called us to dinner, Bing did not appear. We all waited patiently. My mother believes every meal is a celebration of life, a little fiesta, so the table must be set with flowers and candles, and we have to sit down at the table together and have conversations. On Sunday nights we just hang out and eat soup or toasted sandwiches on trays in front of the telly but this was not a Sunday night, and Bing, usually the first to arrive for meals, was nowhere to be seen.

'Bingy, come and get it,' yelled Vera. Bing came slowly down the stairs in her yellow overalls, with the manicure scissors sticking out of her top pocket.

'Look, I cut my hair myself,' she announced cheerfully.

'Oh no!' said Vera. We all stared at Bing. Her hair was cut very short and very unevenly. It looked quite good, actually, all funny lengths and textures, like a wonky poodle.

'Oh my God,' said Vera. 'Bing, how could you?'

'It's good,' Bing answered forcefully, her cherub face screwed up ready for battle. 'Get a grip, Vera. It's my hair and it's cool, okay?'

Vera swallowed. There was a long silence. You could see all my mother's ideas about fabulously good parenting cavorting around inside her head like a dancing flea circus. I held my breath. Josh stared at the pepper grinder. Vera swallowed again.

'Who wants some chicken risotto?' she asked. 'I found this gorgeous Reggiano Parmigiano today, it's just superb.'

An ocean wave of relief rolled across the table and out into the twilight as we all settled down to eat our dinner. Sometimes the Bing-and-Vera Show can get a little wild. When they start yelling at each other you wish you were on a planet where all harsh sounds were outlawed. The day that Vera tried to get Bing to sit at the table until she finished her dinner is a day I would rather forget. Anyhow, that kind of explains Bing for you, except that I haven't mentioned the animals yet.

~~~

Bing is a big-time animal lover. When she was three years old she used to hunt around in the garden for dead beetles and snails. She called them my 'teeny weeny babies' and she tucked them carefully into matchbox beds, on cottonwool mattresses with rose petals for blankets. Next there was Dorothy, a yellow and green budgie, who lost a lot of feathers and died of an icky disease. Then came Eggleton, who is sort of the family cat and sort of Bing's cat. Eggleton is a slender black creature with a bent tail and a sneaky disposition. Well, that's what I think, anyway, but Bing adores him. She had a tank of goldfish for a while but that didn't work out very well because she tended to be over-generous with the dried fish food. The two lucky survivors were sold in our garage sale when we shifted to the house in the hills.

I like our house. It's big and friendly, with windows that look out into a wilderness of trees. When we shifted in, my father painted the rooms in strong colours: rich blue, dusky pink, leafy green. The walls are bright with paintings and drawings and photographs. My favourite is a pastel drawing of a wine glass floating in a sea of joyous yellow and purple and turquoise scribble. Now that we had a large garden Bing begged for a dog, but Vera absolutely refused. Finally, in a compensatory gesture, she said Bing could have guinea pigs.

Personally, I think a dog would have been better. Guinea pigs are heaps of work and can be smelly. Also, you can't take a guinea pig for a walk, well not a very long one, anyway. You're supposed to have a pair of guinea pigs, because one gets lonely, but when Vera said yes Bing went straight to our local paper and, as if it was meant to be, there was the ad.

GUINEA PIG AND HUTCH. FREE TO GOOD HOME.

Vera said Bing could start with one guinea pig, and if she looked after it properly she could get another one later. So that's how we got Begonia. Bing loved her immediately and insisted on carrying the squirming blob in her arms all the way home instead of in the cardboard box. The people who sold her to us called her Mrs Fluffy. 'There's no way I'm calling her that,' said Bing.

We took the guinea pig with us the next time we went to visit Lewis. The day felt special, like a birthday. The temporarily nameless creature munched happily on the grass under the oak tree while we discussed names. Vera suggested Marmalade, because of the orange-brown fur. Bing said that was too obvious. Josh thought Hutchinson would be a good name for a creature who lived in a hutch. 'Duh,' said Bing. I suggested Madonna because it was so silly. No one even bothered to reply. Lewis was still thinking it over.

Bing spent ages checking out the pig's nether regions, and when she was absolutely sure that she owned a girl-pig she chose the name Begonia. She nearly called it Cornflake but everyone thought Begonia was better. Vera made up a little song to celebrate. 'Begonia, Begonia, the fabulous creature from Patagonia,' she sang. Usually I feel embarrassed when my mother sings, and wish she didn't try so hard to seem young and funky, but that day her singing felt just right. Josh made Begonia a daisy-chain necklace and we all sat around lazily in the sun and finished off the chocolate mud cake. Begonia ended up with a tiny sticky brown moustache, and Josh found a two-dollar coin that someone had dropped in the grass.

Even Lewis seemed happier that day.

Bing loved Begonia and did all the stuff you have to do to keep a guinea pig happy, which is quite a lot really. You have to clean the cage and brush the fur, and take your pig out to play in the sun. We fenced off a grassy area of the garden to make an enclosure and put in a log for Begonia to gnaw, a pipe to run through, and some rocks to play on. Bing painted red and yellow daisies on the hutch, and Josh sorted through his collection of bizarre plastic stuff and donated a Day-Glo castle, a family of green plastic frogs and a broken Rubik's Cube. Vera kept meaning to take Bing to the pet shop to get a companion pig but Begonia was so pampered and petted she didn't seem lonely, so it never quite happened.

Bing loved fussing around, doing stuff like trimming the tiny claws when they got scratchy. Then she would settle down on the couch to watch television with Begonia on her lap.

Together they nibbled tiny pieces of pear and carrot and other crunchy stuff, all snuggled up as happy as happy could be.

It was nice to see Bing cheerful now that she had Begonia to fuss over. We'd all been kind of gloomy since Lewis got ill.

here comes summer

The weeks went by and the weather got hotter. The water in our swimming pool was green and slimy. The jobs my father usually did weren't getting done. The azaleas out the front were brown from lack of watering, and the fan in the bathroom was making an annoying clunking sound. Vera kept saying she would get someone in to clean the pool, and then she kept forgetting. In the end I phoned The Pool Doctor myself, so that we could swim. 'Bec, you are an angel,' Vera said, but I didn't want to be an angel. I wanted my father to come home and talk to me about architecture, and photography, and let me practise my French on him. *'Je suis Bec. J'adore les croissants. Ou est la plume de ma tante?'*

I remember lying on the hot concrete by the pool in my tatty old bathers. My head was full of darkness. Unwanted thoughts came marching in like a platoon of dirty shoes. What if I went mad? What if it ran in our family and I was next? What if I shaved my brother's head in the night, forgot how to count, started dribbling my food? What if I got lost on a long dark highway and never found my way home again? I scribbled on the concrete with a wet finger, and tried not to think about anything.

On the surface things were going okay at our house, but they weren't really. Vera brought home special food to cheer us up—stuff she wouldn't usually let us eat, like Pringles, and fish and chips.

Food is one sort of medicine, but when you're troubled eating is not an answer; it just feels like you are stuffing food in on top of your feelings. You can't wipe out sadness with potato crisps. The thing that annoyed me the most was that we weren't supposed to talk about what was happening. It was as though there was some sort of unwritten law that said, Pretend You Are Fine Even Though You Are Not Fine. Vera wouldn't even say the word breakdown or depression. She always said 'your father's illness', as though naming it was too dreadful.

Bing seemed sort of okay, but I worried about Josh. He spent hours on the computer, and he didn't share his facts with us any more. Vera was busy with a new cookbook called *Fabulous Feasts*. She looked pale, and even thinner, and drank a glass of chardonnay as soon as she got in the door each evening, and another two with dinner. Our grandmother was the queen of gin-and-tonic and ended up dying of liver disease, so Vera and her chardonnay scared me. When my mother drank she became very chirpy, but there was a brittle edge to her sparkle, and the next day at breakfast she was best avoided. I remember the day she snapped at me out of the blue when I was trying to find my French book. 'For God's sake, Bec, get a move on.' She didn't help me look for the book or anything.

I remember how no one ever sat in my father's green leather armchair.

<center>~~~</center>

When I'm unhappy I mooch. I like to mooch and make things. I cut stuff from glossy magazines and make pictures. With my scissors and glue I make entire worlds, worlds of cherries and horses and jugglers and roses and palm trees and angels and hearts. At school I hung out with my friends, but after school I stayed in my room, cutting and sticking and drifting and dreaming.

Everyone has different ways of coping with the dark times. Vera is a keep-busy type of person. So is Bing. She invited Megan Murphy, her freckly friend, over to play every day after school. They made little tea parties, and dressed Eggleton and Begonia in dolls' clothes. Begonia didn't seem to mind, but let me tell you that a cat definitely does not take kindly to wearing a green satin bow on its head.

One good thing that happened was that Josh made friends with a funny old guy who lived nearby in a messy cottage with a messy garden. Josh met him one day when the tyre on his bike split. Mr Patrick stopped weeding his garden and came to help. They had a long conversation about rabbits, apparently.

Mr Patrick has done all sorts of jobs in his lifetime, like radio announcer, engineer and milkman. Vera calls him the original greenie because he makes his own yoghurt and sprouts, and he lives on porridge, stuff from his garden, and what he calls 'Everything Stew'. Mr Patrick never throws anything away. His place is cluttered with old newspapers and magazines, tobacco tins, books, records and watch-making equipment. He does odd jobs that no one else can be bothered with, like fixing toasters.

Josh began going down to the cottage, spending dusty hours helping Mr Patrick fix things, drinking milky tea and hearing stories about the old days. Josh said he wasn't sure if all the stories were exactly true but he liked them anyway.

Josh found a kindred spirit in Mr Patrick and I didn't worry about him as much after that. One day he got a school report with an A for everything, like he usually does, but he got a really bad grade for Physical Education. 'D-', it said, in insulting black ink, and the comment read, 'Josh is a great help with shifting the equipment'.

'Well, you know, Physical Education is not really *that* important in the grand scheme of things,' Mr Patrick said. 'I bet Einstein and Mozart were not that good at soccer.'

The worried look in Josh's eyes was replaced by a grin. Josh would have to be the least sporty person I know. His favourite sport is inventing bizarre new email addresses, like iamking@zednet or volkswagonsruletheuniverse@hotmail.com.

on we go

Vera worked hard, cooked softly and drank wine.

Bing dressed Begonia as a baby and a bride. Eggleton hid under the house.

I was the Goddess Queen of a Paper Universe where only good things ever happened.

Josh hung out in a musty world of impossible stories.

The days unfolded, each one following the next, neat as origami.

There was never a turning point. It was like a garden growing, you don't notice it, yet it happens. Slowly my father began to get better. He started telling us about interesting stuff he had read in the architectural magazines. He chomped into the goodies Vera baked for him, instead of just politely nibbling. When Josh asked Vera when Dad was coming home Vera said 'soon', instead of 'I don't know'.

When we got the news that Lewis was coming home Vera went into a frenzy. She bought Turkish bread and nectarines, camembert and prosciutto. She arranged masses of pink roses in her best blue glass vase. There was a red gerbera in the bathroom, and a new cactus in the courtyard. We found out on Friday that Lewis was to come home on Monday, so the entire weekend was a whirlwind of activity.

'Blitz your bedrooms, kids,' Vera insisted. 'We have to get everything really nice for your father.'

There is no point arguing with my mother when she goes

into Frantic Action Mode. 'Yes', we said, and mainly ignored her. Bing made her bed for once, Josh shoved most of his plastic stuff under the bed and the rest of it into the wardrobe. I picked up all my dirty clothes and emptied my rubbish bin, which seemed like a good idea as the three apple cores in it were grey-green and furry to the point of being alive again. Then I sat on my bed with the door closed and wrote my French vocabulary into a notebook, a task which I'd left for too long and could leave for no longer without incurring Mrs Tait's wrath.

A token gesture is all I ever do when Vera gets into her Tidy Your Bedroom Mood, even though this was an important occasion. Let's face it, Lewis couldn't give a toss, he would just be glad to be home, away from the other troubled people and the sharp hospital smell of disinfectant mixed with sorrow. Actually I don't have a concept of mess, I prefer to think of it as creative clutter; layers of stuff to be discarded and rediscovered on a need-to-know basis.

~~~~

On Sunday night we vegged out together in the lounge to watch *The Secret Garden*. I'd seen it before at the movies but it was pretty good the second time around.

'Mmm, gardens, I absolutely must do something about our courtyard,' Vera said vaguely. She gets vague when she is really tired.

'Maybe Daddy will be able to do the courtyard,' Bing said.

'Maybe, Bing Bang,' Vera replied. 'Daddy might even go back to work soon, but we can't rush things, we'll just have to wait and see.'

Fixing The Courtyard was another thing that was on Vera's Must Do List. The man who owned the house before us was a mining engineer who was away a lot. He had let the property get pretty run down. It didn't matter much in the garden, which just looked sort of wild and green and interesting, but the courtyard was a mess. The pavers were cracked and weeds were growing up through the splits. There were some ugly pots with daggy plants here and there, and the whole area had a desolate feel to it. The only nice things in it were the cactus collection and a terracotta statue of a beast with wings that Lewis had been given by a sculptor friend.

'Gardens, houses and kids . . . oh, lovely, lovely but such a very lot of work,' said my mother. I think the Chardonnay had gone to her head—she says the weirdest stuff sometimes. 'Come on, let's go to bed, tomorrow is a big huge day,' said Vera, and for once none of us bothered to argue.

not your average day

The next morning Vera raved on, with her endless list of instructions. The more stressed she gets, the more orders she gives. I wish they had taught her How To Chill at The Cunning Mother Training School.

'I'll be home around six, depending on the traffic. I'm picking up the new book at four and your father at five. It will be so great to have Lewis home, and I can't wait to see the book. How come everything always happens at once? I must remember to phone my agent, I should have done that on Thursday. Now Bing, don't invite anyone over this afternoon, okay? And don't mess up the lounge room. Josh, come straight home and do your homework, get some of your Brazil project done—you haven't done any for ages—and give Bingy a hand with a major blitz of Begonia's cage. Don't just take the paper out this time, disinfect it underneath, it smells a bit pongy. Bec, I've taken this lasagna out of the freezer, bung it in the oven at five-thirty, and whip up a bit of a salad. There's all sorts of stuff in the crisper, use up the asparagus, will you, it's going a bit strange.'

It was a relief to get away from Vera when she was in Control-A-Go-Go Mode. Cycling along, away from her speedy energy, felt great, but I couldn't concentrate that day at school. In English we were studying *The Caucasian Chalk Circle*. Mr Buckley went into one of his impassioned political raves, so I put on my interested face and spent my time doodling hearts on the inside of my folder cover. French was okay until Mrs Tait sprang a vocabulary test on us for the next day. At lunchtime I sat with my friends behind the Science Block. Lisa thought she might be pregnant, but she thought that every month so none of us get excited about it any more.

We lecture her about condoms and the pill and she never takes any notice. She is so nuts. Katherine told us in infinite detail about a gorgeous Japanese guy she met at the beach, and Julia thought of a thousand ways to con her mother out of fifty dollars so she could buy a satin skirt at Lick.

I lay on my back and looked at the sky and said 'mmm' every five minutes, which is my usual contribution when I need to space out. I was missing Eloise, my best friend. Last year her mother got a job teaching drama in New York and the whole family shifted to Brooklyn. I really missed Eloise. Julia and Katherine are both great, but they tend to hang out together a lot. Lisa is more of a loner, I never felt like she really wanted to be that close with me.

I hadn't met Jaz yet, she came later. Talk about weird threads, because if I hadn't met Jaz I would never have . . . but that all happened later and right now I have to tell you what happened about Begonia.

After lunch we had a double period of Human Biology. Miss Scarfe asked me the difference between a vein and an artery, and my mind went completely blank. 'Planet Earth calling Bec, is anybody home?' she asked sarcastically and everybody sniggered. I smudged ink all over my schematic diagram of the circulatory system. Gregory Mallory let off a couple of really smelly farts. It was not a good afternoon.

I rode home feeling restless and fragile. An artery carries blood away from the heart and a vein carries blood to the heart. As if I didn't know that. Now I couldn't remember whether lasagna was supposed to go in a hot oven or a medium oven. I didn't like the world, or myself. My body felt all fidgety. I wanted to be calm and happy because Lewis was coming home, but instead I was anxious and crabby.

That's what I hate about feelings. They're like some mysterious weather that you can't control. Black clouds and wild rainstorms come when you least expect them, rising up out of nowhere. The good thing, I guess, is that the joy times roll up in their own mysterious way as well. What comes next is always a surprise.

~~~

That afternoon was a surprise, and that's for sure. I pedalled furiously up the hill. Went inside. Poured myself a big glass of cold orange juice. Looked in the fridge for something to eat. Found some leftover potato salad and ate it from the container with my fingers. Looked out the window. Major shock. There were Bing and Megan, mucking around on the lawn. They were tying something pink and lacy that looked suspiciously like a pair of underpants on top of Begonia's head.

'Bing, come in here,' I yelled through a mouthful of mayonnaise and potato. 'I mean it, Bing. Immediately, or else.'

When Bing and Megan came inside I didn't know what to say. I like Megan. She's a podgy kid with a crooked smile and an amazing cloud of ginger hair. It was tricky. Vera had said that Megan wasn't to come over, but how could I send her home when she was smiling at me so trustingly?

'Bing, you know what Vera said,' I began.

'No,' said Bing innocently. I didn't know if she had really forgotten or was deliberately being a smarty-pants. It was hard to know with Bing.

'Where's Josh?' I asked. He should have been home by now but his bike wasn't in the shed.

'Dunno,' said Bing. 'Can we go and play now?'

'No,' I answered crossly. 'You absolutely can't. You can help me with the cooking.'

I was thoroughly flustered by now. I had no idea what I was saying. Sometimes it's a drag being the oldest.

'I *love* cooking,' said Megan. 'My mum never lets me.'

That was cool. By mistake, I had come up with a good idea. I didn't want to be the enemy. I wanted to be Nice Older Sister. Maybe cooking would be fun.

'Let's make a cherry almond cake for Dad. It's his favourite.'

Vera doesn't let us cook much. She likes to be Queen of the Kitchen. Sometimes Josh and Bing make pancakes on Sunday mornings. Lewis produces a yummy Thai chicken curry once in a while, leaving the kitchen in total chaos. I mainly put things in the oven and make salads. However, since I had an entire afternoon and two eager helpers at my disposal, perhaps I could wear Vera's crown, or at least her apron.

So I put on the soft blue floral apron and the three of us

began to cook. Megan beat the butter and sugar, Bing sifted the dry ingredients, and I rummaged around in the pantry looking for cooking chocolate, rum essence and a jar of sour cherries, which fortunately we had. It was such fun that I forgot all about Josh until he suddenly appeared, just as we were triumphantly putting the cake into the oven.

'Where on earth have you been? You know Vera said to come straight home.'

'Well, I did, sort of. I only went to Mr Patrick's to get this *National Geographic* magazine. It has an article in it about Brazil, and he said I can keep it and cut out the pictures for my project. And guess what? His son just sent him a great big book about scientists. Did you know that Edmund Halley, the astronomer who discovered the comet, also invented the diving suit? He was into opium as well. Mr Patrick told me all about it. Opium comes from a poppy, which is interesting because poppies are red and opium is white.'

'That's all very well, but Vera did say to come straight home.'

I could never get properly angry with Josh. He was too skinny and innocent, like some kind of soft animal or flower bud.

'Help, it's five o'clock. Megan, you'd best go home now. Bing and Josh, bring Begonia inside and clean her cage, *thoroughly*, like Vera said. Then Josh, you do your homework and Bing, you come and set the table. Now, scoot, I have to do something with the asparagus.

'You sound just like Vera,' said Bing. 'You'd better do the asparagus, Bec, before we *all* go strange.'

~~~

Just as I was getting the salad stuff out of the fridge I heard screaming. I ran outside. Josh stood there, absolutely still. Bing was crying and yelling so hard that I couldn't make out any words. There was only a big garble of sound and tears. I remember looking for blood, thinking that maybe one of them had cut themselves. Snakebite? Oh, God, please don't let it be snakebite.

'What is it? What's happening?' I grabbed Bing and hugged her to me. Josh spoke. His face was pale as a cloud.

'It's Begonia. She's gone.'

At first I felt relief. At least it wasn't a Category A Disaster. Category A is when your house burns down or someone you love is dead or dying. This was more of a Category B Disaster, which includes losing your boyfriend, your purse or your guinea pig.

Bing stopped sobbing and settled down enough to tell me what had happened. When she and Megan hurried inside they had left the gate open, and now Begonia was nowhere to be seen. I felt as guilty as hell. It might not be a Category A Disaster to me but it was to Bing, and if I hadn't called her in so crossly maybe she would have remembered to shut the gate. There was no time for regret. We had to find Begonia before some mean dog did.

The three of us hunted everywhere. Somehow I remembered to put the lasagna into the oven and take the cake out at the right time. I bunged all the salad stuff in a bowl. Forget Queen of the Kitchen. This was desperate. We kept hunting: under the house, in the shed, down the driveway. Josh scoured the vacant land next door. Bing crawled around under the hedge, calling and calling, 'Where are you, little friend?'

~~~

Six o'clock. Vera and Lewis drove in right on time. My father looked tall and strong and handsome. All my feelings were muddled together. I couldn't bear to say anything but Vera knew something was wrong, so I had to tell them what had happened. We all searched but we couldn't find Begonia. When the light began to fade there was no point searching any longer so we came in for dinner.

We tried so hard to be cheerful that night.

'Superb lasagna, my angel,' said Lewis. 'You guys can't imagine how good it is to be home with my beautiful family.'

'The cake is gorgeous and the salad was lovely, Bec,' said Vera. 'Well done. Bing, honey, Begonia will turn up, I know she will.'

'Yeah, maybe,' said Bing. It cost her a lot to say that. You could tell that she really wanted to be angry and rude, because she was hurting so much, but our father had come home, and Bing didn't want to spoil things.

'Mr Patrick told me about Anton van Someone-or-Other—

I've forgotten his name—but he was Dutch and he was the first scientist to use a microscope,' said Josh, trying to fill the awkward silence. 'Guess what?' my brother continued. 'He used to put all sorts of weird stuff under his lens, like the tiny insides of honey bees, and wee.'

'Was it bee wee or people wee?' asked Bing, perking up slightly. 'People wee,' said Josh. 'And semen.'

'What's semen?' asked Bing.

'Right,' said Vera firmly. 'Why don't you guys go do your homework and Daddy and I will clear the table. When we've got the dishes sorted I'll make us some coffee, and bring you kids some hot chocolate.'

'What's semen?' Bing insisted.

'Semen is not a good subject for right now. I'll tell you when I tuck you into bed later,' side-stepped Vera. 'Come on, buzz off.'

'Buzz buzz buzz like a honey bee, like bee wee, like . . .'

'Scram,' said Vera, in her special Vera voice that means if you don't obey you'll get a major blasting.

'I don't have homework, can I watch *The Simpsons*?' Bing asked. Vera has a thing about *The Simpsons* being gross and ghastly but that night she just threw up her hands and said yes.

Lewis blew out the candles and began to take the dirty plates into the kitchen.

'Superb cake, Bec, really, I think I'll have another bit with my coffee.'

'Thanks, Dad. I've got a French test tomorrow, I'd better try and cram in a verb or two,' I answered, and went slowly upstairs.

My backpack felt as heavy as lead. Josh came up with me, carrying his *National Geographic* magazine. I went into my bedroom and threw myself down onto my patchwork bed-spread. I love my bed. It is my ultimate comfort zone. Safe cosy squishy comfy bed. My room was chaotic. Not that I would ever admit that to Vera.

STEP ONE: Bung all the stuff from my desk on to the floor.

STEP TWO: Look in the mirror and check out what my hair looks like. Show great restraint and do not pick the tiny pimple on my chin.

STEP THREE: Ask God why what was meant to be a good day turned out so crappy.

STEP FOUR: Find my goddamn vocab book. *Je suis* pooped. No, ! had better make that *je suis absolument* pooped.

Just then Bing started screaming.

Josh and I almost fell over each other trying to get down the stairs. Lewis and Vera and Bing were in the middle of the lounge in a big huddle. Bing was bawling her eyes out.

'Hey, steady on, we don't want to squash her,' Lewis said loudly.

What was he on about? Bing is the least squashable kid on the planet.

If a memory can have a colour this one is rose gold, like in a dreamy movie. In a slow, clumsy lounge room tango, my parents stepped back and there between them was Bing. Clutched in her arms was Begonia.

'She was under the couch! Begonia was asleep under the couch,' yelled Bing. She burst into tears again but these were joy tears. 'You are a naughty naughty wonderful pig,' Bing sniffled.

Vera made hot chocolate, there was lots more hugging and we all went to bed.

everything changes

It was a time of purple. Jacaranda trees with soft purple blossoms. Sitting on the back step with Lewis, a carpet of drifty petals under our feet, pretending to be philosophers, having silly conversations half in English and half in French. Violet Crumble bars at lunchtime with Lisa, Katherine and Julia, as we invented wildly wonderful futures for ourselves. Pale creamy lilac for the dress Vera wore to the launch of her new book, *Fabulous Feasts*.

Christmas came and went. Vera did her usual extravaganza of elegant cooking. We ate chicken with rosemary, tiny new potatoes, rocket salad with shaved parmesan and artichoke hearts, followed by nectarines in brandy with double cream. Sometimes having a celebrity cook for a mother can be tiresome, but sometimes it tastes just fine.

We drank champagne. Vera put heaps of orange juice in Josh's and Bing's but she poured mine straight from the bottle, into a proper crystal flute, and added a strawberry. It was crispy cold and fizzly. My legs went all goofy and happy, and so did I. Mr Patrick came for lunch, bringing Josh a gift of a very old *Botanical Encyclopaedia*, with exquisite engravings of plants, seeds and flowers.

I got heaps of neat pressies: a Ben Harper CD, twenty dollars, a white satin nighty, a chocolate heart, two vanilla scented candles and four books.

It was hot. We swam in the pool. We lay in the shade and read our Christmas presents. Then it was Boxing Day.

'Whew,' said Vera. 'I'm glad that's over.'

I was glad, too. Now it was time to do nothing but enjoy myself for four whole weeks.

~~~

Summer is every colour. Blue for sky and blue for ocean. Turquoise for swimming pool. Pale green for grapes. Summer is as yellow as butter smeared on sweet corn; as yellow as Bing's funny hair bleached by the sun. Red for wrapping paper and strawberries and Vera's toenails. Bright orange for my new bathing suit. White for the hottest part of the day. Silver for playing my flute under a tree at palest sunset.

The school holidays seemed to go on for ever. I slept in every single day. Went to the pool with Lisa, dipping and diving in my new cossie. Katherine and I went to see *The Spy*

Who Shagged Me. It was hell-funny. Couldn't get together with Julia cos she was out of town. Slept in some more. Made popcorn and watched funny videos with Josh and Bing. Went to the library and got out heaps of magazines, and seven books. Lay on my bed and read for the entire afternoon. Vera took a few days off and we all went down south to Margaret River. We walked on the beach and swam in the ocean. We buried Lewis in the sand, so that only his head was showing. We sculpted sand mermaids, giving them shell necklaces and pink seaweed hair. We played Scrabble and Monopoly and Cluedo and Boggle and Poker and Cheat. We had chocolate croissants for breakfast and lazy picnics under shady trees. We were happy like a family again.

~~~

Suddenly the holidays were over and it was time to go back to school. Everything felt sort of familiar and sort of strange. We covered our exercise books with contact paper, and complained when it got bubbles in it, just like we did every year. We hunted for our schoolbags in cluttered cupboards. Vera bustled around organising sandwiches, muesli bars, and frozen orange juice. Old familiar lunch boxes. New socks. New felt-tip pens. We were ready.

The first day of school was chaos, a general muddle of timetables and book lists and room changes. The corridors smelled of sweaty feet and ninety-seven sorts of body spray. The teachers looked like they wished they were still in

Broome or in Bali, anywhere but back with the noisy Year Elevens and a mountain of text books to sort out.

At lunchtime I made for our favourite spot under the trees to hang out with Julia, Katherine and Lisa. We scrabbled around in our backpacks for our lunches and did a bit of swapping. Other people's lunches are always more interesting than your own. For example, Julia's mother makes yummy ham rolls, but Julia is a sugar freak so she trades her rolls for my boring muesli bars. Katherine only brings fruit, because she thinks she's fat, but then she's ravenous and eats everything in sight.

While we ate we caught up on all the gossip. Julia was in a snitch because she came to school with glitter all over her face and Mrs Tait made her remove it. Katherine was still madly in love and in lust with Kenzo.

'Guess what?' she blurted out. 'I actually did it! I lost my vees.'

At first I didn't have a clue what she was talking about. Lost her 'vees'? Then it dawned on me, she meant she had lost her virginity. Holy shmoley! I'd always thought Katherine would be the least likely of us to have sex. I didn't know what to say.

Lisa did, though. 'I hope you used contraception,' she drawled, with a big smirk on her face. 'Seeing you always tell meeeeee to.' Katherine blushed bright pink and changed the topic as fast as she could. Lisa finished looking smug and sat back looking bored and dreamy. 'Where did the holidays go?' she muttered. 'I wanna go home.'

The afternoon dragged by. I remember cycling home after school that day in the fierce dry heat. I was wondering what it actually felt like, doing it with a guy. It felt weird to even think about it. I mean, I know all the facts and everything, which bit goes where, and how not to get preggie, but when it came to imagining what it really felt like . . . I didn't even want to go there. Thinking about anything in that heat was tiring but especially *that*. Sweat was running down my neck, and my legs could hardly pedal. The grass on the nature reserve was dead and scratchy. I was looking forward to getting my feet out of my sandals, to the cool wet embrace of the pool.

Vera and Lewis were sitting at the kitchen table.

'Hello, doll, how was it?' asked my father.

'Hot and grotty mainly, but yeah, okay, I guess. I've still got Mrs Tait for French and Mr Buckley for English. Miss Scarfe left, so now we've got Mr Palmer for Science, he's kind of all right.'

As I poured myself some cold water from the carafe in the fridge, I glanced at Vera. She was wearing a black singlet and a green sarong. Her hair was piled on top of her head in a tumble of curls. Her shoulders were bony and fragile. It might sound really strange but suddenly I knew something huge was about to happen. I can't explain how I knew, but I did.

I sat down at the table. Vera pushed a bowl of plums

towards me. I wasn't hungry. It was too hot to eat.

'I got a call from my publishers today, Bec,' said Vera. *'Fabulous Feasts* is selling like hot cakes, both in Australia and, get this, in America. They're talking about a further print run, another ten thousand copies!'

'Cool. That's great, Mum. It's such a good book.'

'The thing is . . .' Vera stopped. She picked up a plum and bit into the juicy crimson flesh. A fleck smudged on her chin and she wiped it off with the back of her hand.

'What? What's the thing?' I asked. Vera wouldn't look at me. That was bad. Lewis was silent. I couldn't read his face.

'They've offered me a book tour,' Vera continued. 'Sydney and Melbourne, and then three weeks in the States.'

'God, Mum, that's major. I mean that's fantastic, right?'

'Yes, it is, sweetie. I'm so glad you think so. We thought you might be upset.'

'Why would I be upset?'

I wasn't sure if I *was* upset. I hadn't had time to think about anything yet, but somehow I knew what the required answer was without even having to think. My mouth knew how to do the talking but it didn't actually seem to be linked to my brain.

'Well, it's quite a long time to be away. I mean, we'll be gone for over five weeks and I wasn't sure how you'd feel about that. I mean, we'll get a really good housekeeper and we'll phone you, and bring you home some gorgeous presents. You guys will be just fine while we're away.'

'Housekeeper?'

I changed my mind, grabbed a plum and took a bite. It gave me something to do with my hands while my thoughts and feelings turned cartwheels.

'Darling, you know we couldn't leave you here without an adult. I mean, you're so great with Bing and Josh but you're only fifteen . . .'

'It's a brilliant opportunity for your mother . . .' said Lewis, sounding anxious.

'Daddy needs this, too,' Vera butted in. 'Having some time away will be just the best thing. We could both do with it after all that's happened lately. We're even going to have a week's holiday at the end. We haven't decided where yet. Maybe New Mexico. We've always dreamt of going there. We wanted to tell you first, before Bing and Josh came home. Oh Bec, I'm so glad you understand. I was so worried about your reaction.'

My parents had stopped talking and were looking at me. The afternoon felt like an itchy blanket all around me. I could taste summery plum in my mouth. I didn't know what to say, or what to think. Somehow an important moment had slipped right past me, like a wisp of silk scarf, and I hadn't had time to grab it. An image came into my mind, a video clip from the dark recesses of nowhere. I saw a big bus pulling away from me, leaving me standing alone at the bus stop. The girl who was Bec wanted to call out 'Hey, hang on. Don't go without me', but it was too late. The bus was vanishing out of sight.

I didn't want my parents to go away. Not so soon after Lewis had come home. Not without me and Josh and Bing. I certainly didn't want some weird housekeeper in our home. No way. But I couldn't say anything now. It was too late. I had to pretend it was fine.

Maybe it would be fine. That was what I told myself. Yes, it would be fine. Lewis and Vera would only be gone for five weeks. That wasn't very long. I could deal with it. Except for the housekeeper bit. I didn't like the thought of some stranger bossing us around. I kept getting this picture in my mind of the guy in *Mrs Doubtfire*, wearing heaps of make-up, a padded bra and silly high-heeled shoes. Get a grip, Bec, I told myself. Whoever the housekeeper is, it certainly won't be Robin Williams dressed as a woman. This is not a dumb movie. This is real life.

I went up to my bedroom, slamming the door just loudly enough to worry my parents yet not quite drastically enough to bring one of them upstairs, and sprawled face down on the bed. 'Fuck Fuck Fuck Fuck Fuck', I said, because the word is forbidden in our house. I said it loudly, but I didn't feel any better. I was furious with my mother. Selfish old cow, her and her bloody book tour and her agent and her *me me me*. Vera the celebrity. Vera the famous. Vera the pain in the bum.

Maybe it sounds strange, but being angry with Vera was so

familiar it felt almost comfortable. My mother's faults were so obvious. She was impatient and self-centred and neurotic, like a child whose needs always came first. Sometimes I totally despised her, and often I wished she were more of a mother and less of a star turn, but Vera was just Vera. She was flawed but she was also special: flamboyant, lively, interesting. It wasn't always easy but way down deep I loved my mother and I knew she loved me, with her scattered busy love. I knew where I stood with Vera. Sometimes she annoyed the hell out of me but I always got over it. What really scared me that day was how angry I felt towards Lewis.

I hated him for not coping; for no longer being the way he once was, steady and dependable and strong. I hated him for not knowing that it was too soon to go away, and for not standing up to my mother and her wild schemes. I hated him because the fan clunked and the azaleas were dying.

So this was growing up. The place where there was no mummy and daddy any more. I shoved my head under the pillow and bit my finger until it hurt, and then I cried.

the dreaded mrs d

I thought Bing would make a fuss when she heard the big news, but she didn't. 'America, wow, cool,' she said. 'Just don't get a yucky person for a housekeeper. Hey, can you bring me some magic sea monkeys from America, because this kid I know told me all about them, his grandfather brought him some. It's like little dried stuff, you put it in water and they come to life. It's bloody amazing.'

'Bing, don't say bloody,' said Vera.

'Oh, piffle,' said Bing. She was already burbling on about something else. 'We're doing All about Me at school. I asked Mr Price if I could bring Begonia along tomorrow and he said I can. I need to get a big carton and make some holes in it. Have we got a big carton, Vera?'

Josh zoomed up the drive, his skinny legs pedalling like mad. Vera waited until he had poured himself a glass of juice and begun his homework. Then she told him the news, bursting with enthusiasm. He didn't think it was such a good idea. I could tell he didn't. He just nodded, and went on colouring in his map of Brazil.

I went upstairs and lay on my bed. Questions went round and round my head; heaps of questions but no answers, thumping around in my brain like an old wheelbarrow. Why did my parents have to go away, just when everything was nearly back to normal? Why did everything have to change? Why did I feel so weird when Katherine told me she lost her vees? How come I didn't even like any of the boys I knew? I couldn't imagine falling in love, or lust, with anyone—certainly not with Gregory Mallory with his hairy legs and his silly jokes, or with Adam Palmer who was sort of good looking but thought he was God's gift to the universe.

~~~

Vera went into Frantic Action Mode big-time, planning the trip. She shopped for an expensive satin toilet bag, two shiny black suitcases with wheels, and a magenta woollen suit to wear when she was being interviewed. She called it My Impress-People-Outfit. There were endless phone calls, glossy brochures about New Mexico, long discussions about which hotel to book in San Francisco. Everything centred around the merits of various Frequent Flyer plans, and handy tips on how to travel light. Each night at dinner the conversation was a flurry of dates and details. It was most exhausting.

Lewis spent most of the day in his study, sorting out his teaching materials and catching up on reading heavy academic stuff. After the trip he was going to go back to his job, teaching at the university. Sometimes I took him a cup of tea, and helped him do stuff like staple hand-outs together. The study was one place that was safe from the clutches of Whirlwind Woman. Lewis and I had one long memorable conversation in which he tried to explain post-structuralism to me, but I didn't really get it. The anti-depressant medication meant my father was almost his old self, but not quite. It was hard to put your finger on the not-quiteness. The only thing I can be specific about was that he was more vague. He would stop halfway through a sentence, as if waiting for the next thought to arrive, and he did things like lose his glasses. We hunted everywhere but in the end he had to buy a new pair.

'I am Lewis-the-nearly-normal,' he joked at dinner.

'Who are we then, Dad?' Bing asked.

'Oh, isn't it obvious? You are Bing-the-batty, Bec-the-madgirl and Josh . . . um . . . Josh-the-jumbled,' my father replied. 'The children of Loony-Lewis and Vera-the-voluptuous.'

'Vera-the-voluptuous indeed,' retorted my mother. 'I might have put on a teensy tiny bit of weight, but it's only because we're doing a special Valentine's Day program about sinful desserts. It's been double cream and chocolate everything at the test kitchen this week. While we're on food, my favourite subject, pass the spinach roulade, would you please, Lewis-the-lovely? It's rather scrummy, isn't it? The fetta and nutmeg give it that extra smidgen of oomph!'

~~~~

Two days later. At school. Lunchtime.

We were stretched out on the benches outside the science lab, me and Lisa and Julia and Jaz. Jaz had just enrolled at our school. The day before, Mrs Louden, my home room teacher, asked me to look after her, so I did. Fortunately I really liked her, and so did my friends. Her real name is Jasmine and she comes from Malaysia. She has dyed her hair post-box red. It looks really bizarre. It's neon-day-glo-plastic-fantastic-red. Follow-me-and-fall-in-love-with-me-red. Jaz is really out there, she's heaps of fun. We were trying to get our legs brown. Brown legs look so cool but they come with a certain amount of guilt. I wish there was no such thing as a hole in the ozone layer or skin cancer.

'Bec, you're so lucky,' Julia announced. 'I wish my parents were going away for a whole month. It would be a relief. My mother just goes on and on about every tiny little thing these days. She can be such a moody old bag. And *America*, that's so cool. Think of the joy prezzies you can ask for.'

'Mmm,' I said. 'I guess . . . it's just that, I don't know, I feel weird about it.'

'Weird like why?' asked Jaz. 'Weird like you want to go too?'

'No, it isn't that. I mean, five of us going would cost heaps, and it'd be really hectic and full-on. Even hearing the itinerary makes me feel tired. "If this is Tuesday it must be Chicago" kind of thing. Just weird because it came out of nowhere. We were just getting back to normal after my father being in hospital and then, *wham*, my parents just sprang it on us. And then there's the housekeeper, Mrs Dempster.'

'Bec, you said they hadn't found one yet. Who on earth is Mrs Dempster?' Lisa can be quite lizard-like; until she spoke I was sure she was asleep. She was right. I hadn't told anyone about Mrs Dempster, because once I said it out loud to my friends it would mean that it was really happening, and I still didn't want it to.

Mrs Dempster works with my mother. She's a food stylist. She does stuff like spray oil on mashed potatoes so they look all creamy and yummy in the photo shoots. 'Food stylist' sounds young and funky but Mrs Dempster is about fifty. Her hair is iron-grey and cut short. She wears baggy rayon dresses and has these big chafed-looking hands. She used to be a home economics teacher, and Vera really likes her because she's so practical and reliable. 'Good old unflappable Mrs D', Vera calls her. To be honest I found her rather dull and plodding. Her first name is Doreen. No wonder she sticks with calling herself Mrs Dempster. Doreen is a name like Maud or Enid or Ivy. An old biddy sort of a name.

I describe her to my friends.

'Ick,' says Lisa.

'You can come over to my place any time you like,' says Jaz.

'Try and make your parents feel really guilty about going and ask for New York stuff. It's the best! Velvet hair flowers. And clear plastic handbags with like, plastic goldfish swimming in them. Make sure they bring you heaps of New York stuff,' says Julia.

'Katherine?' I ask.

'Yeah,' she answers idly, filing her nails with a zappy purple nail file she probably bought in Esprit for about twenty dollars or something.

'What was it like, with Kenzo?'

Katherine stops filing. For a minute I think she isn't going to answer, but then she does.

'It was okay, I guess.'

'Only okay?' asks Lisa. She asked casually, like she didn't really care about the answer, but you could tell she was curious.

'Yeah, it was . . . God, do I really have to tell you . . . I mean Kenzo is a really really nice guy, or I wouldn't have done it, but it was a bit . . . clumsy. I mean it wasn't like in the movies.'

Silence. I want to ask more but I feel like a doofus.

More silence.

'It isn't as easy as a carrot,' says Katherine suddenly. We all stare at her. 'Putting the condom on . . . when you do it in Health Ed, put one on a carrot, it's easy, but in real life . . .'

'Practice makes perfect, baby,' says Lisa, trying to sound sophisticated.

'What about Kenzo?' Julia inquires timidly, 'Couldn't he . . .?'

'Nah, not really,' said Katherine. She started giggling.

My mind was boggling, trying to picture it, then trying not to. I let out a great snort of laughter, and that was that. We spent the rest of lunch break rolling around on the grass having hysterics. Each time one of us stopped laughing someone would blurt out 'not as easy as a carrot' and the laughter would begin again, reaching fever pitch when Gregory Mallory walked past eating a banana. Thank goodness for the siren, or we'd have wet our pants.

I go home feeling most odd. I feel like a drifting cloud. I hide in my bedroom, and watch Bing and Megan from my window. They're wearing big floppy hats from the dress-up box and are trying to make Begonia sit on a little chair, like at a tea party. Begonia won't. She wriggles and tries to run away. I don't blame her. I make up an imaginary newspaper headline which says, 'Guinea pig forced into unnatural acts by evil little girls, claims RSPCA.' Finally Bing and Megan give up and lie down on the grass, giggling like crazy about something. Josh is down at the cottage with Mr Patrick. They're working on a special project, restoring an old juke-box.

I am lonesome and cranky. I get out my stash of old glossy magazines, my scissors and my glue stick. I've got a great big pile of gourmet cooking and lifestyle magazines that Vera has discarded, and some flashy architecture and graphic design ones that Lewis gave me. I love the fabulous photographs of fabulous places, the elegant pictures in which everything is tasteful and perfect. In the paper land there are no zits, no homework, no bustling mothers too busy to ask how your day went, no clumsiness, no condoms, no hard decisions, no lost spectacles. In the paper land there are no sad hearts or emptiness or loss. I begin to make a collage of a thousand flowers. Well, lots of flowers, anyway. I cut out roses and sunflowers and lilies and sweet peas. I worry about my hair for something to do.

WHAT TO DO WITH YOUR HAIR

Stare in the mirror and wish it was different. Brush it.
Wash it. Colour it. Tease it. Talk to it. Burn the split ends
off very carefully with a match. Gel it. Mousse it. Crimp it.
Plait it. Stencil moons and stars on it with hair glitter.
Cut the whole lot off. Make ringlets. Iron it. Stick a hat
on top. Trim the fringe using a piece of sticky tape as
a guide line. Let it go all dreadlocky and weird. Spray it.
Play it. Love it. Leave it. If your mother says it looks
fabulous change it immediately.

sunday the 24th of february 1999

The big day dawned. Well, I guess it dawned. I didn't get up
till ten o'clock and by then it had definitely arrived. I stayed
in bed for as long as I could, floating in and out of sleep,
gliding on the edge of a dream about me and a Mexican highway and a sky-blue car that wouldn't start.

Mrs Dempster drove up after lunch, with three dented
suitcases, a portable fan, and a cheerful here-we-go-team
attitude. She was like the captain of a ship, ready for duty. It's
a wonder she isn't wearing a jaunty little cap on her head
and a sailor's jacket, I thought, meanly, and then felt guilty.
I should probably at least try to like her.

It was a very all-over-the-place afternoon. Bing asked if

she could take Begonia to the airport to say goodbye. Vera squawked. Bing squawked. Vera squawked the loudest. Begonia was not allowed to come. Josh looked pale, like a white sheet that got washed with a black one and came out all grey. Vera went over and over everything a million times, and taped little lists everywhere. She kept hugging us. Lewis misplaced his new spectacles. Then he found them in the shed. 'Oh, my God,' said Vera, 'look at the time.'

We drove to the airport in Mrs Dempster's grey Pajero.

'How come you have this great big four wheel-drive when there's only one of you?' asked Bing.

'Bing, honey,' said Vera.

'No, that's all right,' said Mrs D. 'I need a large vehicle to transport my dogs. I have three greyhounds. They live at a kennel, but when I take them to race they go in a special box, which is pretty big. It only just fits in the back as it is, actually.'

'Wow,' said Bing. 'I loooooove dogs, but Vera won't let me have one.'

'Would you like to come to visit them at the kennel with me next weekend?' asked Mrs D.

'Does a bear shit in the woods?' replied Bing.

'Bing, for goodness' sake!' said Vera.

'No, that's all right,' said Mrs D.

We had arrived at the airport. Thank goodness for that, Josh signalled, by rolling his eyeballs and making a mad monster face. The adults were being particularly strange that afternoon. Sometimes grown-ups are just too bizarre.

Even though it was only a domestic flight to Melbourne the airport was crowded. There were Indian families and Chinese businessmen and Swedish backpackers. Airports are weird places. On one hand they are kind of dull but they have an air of excitement as well. They are in-between places.

Suddenly I wanted to go, too.

'Mummy,' said Bing tearfully, and hid her face in Vera's coat.

'There, there, come along, dear,' said Mrs Dempster, briskly.

After that no one knew what to say. Vera scruffled through her travel documents one last time. Josh went spacey and we couldn't find him. He turned out to be in a shop looking at the whizz-bang electronic stuff like digital cameras.

'Don't forget my sea monkeys,' said Bing.

Vera remembered that she forgot to tell Mrs Dempster about the reticulation system for the garden. Lewis said he had taped a complete set of instructions to the control box. Mrs Dempster said, 'Don't worry, everything will be fine,' ninety-seven times.

Then there were no more minutes left. My parents hugged us each in turn. They walked away on ugly brown airport carpet, vanishing down the narrow corridor where only the passengers are allowed to go. They waved. We waved. They were gone.

~~~

'So,' Mrs D asked as we drove home. 'What do you kids like to eat?'

Silence. I don't know what Bing and Josh were thinking but I was thinking that it was a stupid question, and I had to force myself not to answer, 'Well, food, preferably.' I was staring at Mrs Dempster's hands on the driving wheel; her large sensible hands. I wondered why they were so red and itchy-looking. Maybe she had dermatitis.

'I eat most things,' I volunteered, taking pity on her.

'So do I,' Bing joined in. 'I eat everything except mushrooms, capsicums, olives, pâté, anchovies, pumpkin, silver beet and cooked carrot. I don't like anything green much, except green jelly. I'm fond of chocolate, as long as it's good quality, and I love scrambled eggs the way Vera makes them with smoked salmon and lots of butter and a sprinkling of chives.'

'Indeed,' said Mrs D. 'Well, you *are* a gourmet's daughter, aren't you now.'

More silence.

'So, Joshua, what do you like to eat, or not eat?'

'My name is Josh, not Joshua. Well, I won't eat the eggs of Emperor Penguins,' announced Josh. 'The Emperor Penguin,' he continued, 'is the finest father in the animal kingdom. He carries the egg around for a period of four months, to keep it from touching the ice. You do get the odd accident, of course, where the father penguin drops the egg by mistake, but that's an exception rather than the rule. The Australian seahorse is another really good father. He actually gets pregnant, not the female. I don't eat seahorses either.'

'Oh.' Mrs D took a moment before replying. Her face was as blank as a piece of cardboard. I sneaked a look in the mirror so that I could see what was happening in the back seat. Bing was staring out the window. Josh was smirking.

'That's very interesting, Josh. I must say I wasn't actually thinking of serving penguin eggs or seahorses for dinner tonight. I thought I might make a pizza.'

'Pizza is good,' said Bing. 'Pizza is excellent.'

~~~~~

When we got home Bing, Josh and I headed straight for Josh's bedroom. Bing curled up in the beige vinyl beanbag that Vera found in an op shop and just *had* to have. She reckoned it was classic sixties. I sprawled out on the bed. Josh has a horrible bedspread, a gloomy dark-blue fake tartan, but his mattress is nice and bouncy. Apart from the bedspread, I love my brother's room. There are posters of dolphins and tigers on the wall, and bright transparent stickers on the window of mandalas and ancient Celtic runes. His shelves hold a collection of fossils and rocks and shells. Josh has some seriously nice things, like a seahorse floating in a bottle of murky purple liquid, and a South American sand picture of a house and a palm tree, delicately created from vivid layers of coloured sand. Rows of *National Geographic* and *Omni* magazines and encyclopaedias are arranged in an orderly fashion, and so is his desk, with a jar of pens, the *Far Side* desk calendar that Lewis bought him for Christmas, and a framed picture of Albert Einstein.

Josh sat at his desk, looking pretty much like a younger Albert E. His face was kind of owly behind his spectacles, and he needed a hair cut.

'"Emperor Penguins" indeed, Josh, that was absolutely wicked,' I said. I couldn't help laughing.

'Yeah, well,' said Josh. 'She treats us like we're about seven.'

'I think you're both being horrible,' said Bing. 'Mrs Dempster is nice. She has greyhounds.'

'Yes, well, Hitler liked cats,' I retorted. 'It didn't make him a very wonderful person.'

'Very true,' said Josh.

'Mrs Dempster isn't Hitler. I like her. You guys are just being mean. Anyhow, we have to live with her for ages, so we might as well get along.'

Bing is way too intelligent for her age. She can be irritatingly logical. Sometimes I wish I had a dumber little sister, so I could always be right.

'Well, maybe I *should* like Mrs D but I don't, so there,' I snapped.

Bing smiled at me self-righteously.

'Hitler was a very complex character. He was a vegetarian,'

said Josh, 'and he was a sexual pervert, as well. I watched a program about him on TV.'

'What's a pervert?' asked Bing.

'A weirdo,' said Josh. 'Actually I don't know. Ask Bec.'

'Come and get it,' yelled Mrs D.

Saved by the pizza. I have many talents but explaining sexual perversion to my little sister is not one of them. What would I know, anyhow? Even kissing someone sounds a bit slobbery to me. I'm just not into boys and that is that.

~~~

The pizza was good. It had a thin crispy crust and was topped with melted mozzarella, artichoke hearts, ham and pineapple. At least her cooking was okay.

'Let's watch *The Simpsons*,' said Mrs D.

I could see Bing open her mouth to say we weren't allowed to, and then quickly close it again. She and Josh plonked down beside Mrs D on the sofa to watch the show, but I went upstairs. If Doreen the Dreadful thought she could buy me with pizza she was wrong. I was really pissed off with her for saying 'a gourmet's daughter' in such a sneering way. There's nothing the matter with being a gourmet, I told myself, but deep down I knew Mrs D had touched something squelchy, the part of me that found Vera's food obsession a bit of a wank. I rang Jaz and talked for forty-seven and a half minutes. Then I rang Julia but she wasn't home, so I was forced to do my homework. Life is tough.

the first week

When I try to remember everything that happened back then the colours are tangled together, as if Begonia got into the basket of wool and tumbled among the skeins until they were a complete muddle. Bits and pieces. Fragments like bright shiny pebbles, like broken glass. That's what I remember.

ONE: Bing bought a turtle from a kid at school. She didn't ask if she could, she just did. It cost ten bucks, which included the tank and half a container of turtle food. Mrs Dempster ummed and ahhed a bit but in the end she let Bing keep him. The turtle's name is Theodore.

TWO: I went into the garden to practise my flute and I saw something glinting amongst the nasturtiums. It was the pair of spectacles that Lewis had lost, not the pair he misplaced the day he left, but the pair he *really* lost. I put them on top of a fence post and they watched me, a pair of friendly eyes, as I played *Blue Moon* rather badly. My flute playing was a bit dodgy because I didn't practise often enough. I took the spectacles inside and put them carefully on my father's desk, where they would be safe until he returned.

THREE: Mrs Dempster cooked different foods from Vera; things like mashed potato with lots of butter, and rissoles in gravy, and apricots with custard. She taught Josh how to make Afghan biscuits, with heaps of sugar and butter and cocoa, and chocolate icing and walnuts on top. He took some down to Mr Patrick, who was most impressed.

FOUR: We all went to the kennel to visit the greyhounds. Their names were James Dean, Elmore the Second, and Lucky Star. They were lean, elegant animals with shiny coats. On the way home we had a major junk food pig-out: burgers and Coke and fries.

'This is absolutely bloody delicious,' said Bing.

'I couldn't agree more,' said Mrs Dempster.

FIVE: My parents phoned from Sydney. 'The interview went well. Melbourne was great, and Sydney is really buzzing. We had a fabulous Turkish lunch in Surry Hills, and took a ferry to Manly. This is such a beautiful city. Tomorrow we fly to Los Angeles,' said Vera.

'I miss you guys,' said Lewis.

'Me, too,' yelled Vera from the background.

SIX: Kenzo, the Japanese boy Katherine met at the beach, went home to Tokyo. At first Lisa, Julia, Jaz and I listened sympathetically. That's what friends are for, right, but Katherine can be very dramatic. She tosses words like 'broken heart' and 'my one true love' around as gaily as if they were handfuls of confetti. We were kind and supportive for four whole lunchtimes.

Then Julia said, 'Come on, Katherine. You didn't even know him for very long, and you knew all the time that he had to go back to Japan soon. Get a grip, okay?'

Lisa joined in. 'You knew he was going away and you still decided to lose your vees with him. If you feel bad about it now, well, it's your own fault. Anyway, it's done now, so get over it.'

Katherine looked hurt. She opened her mouth to say something and then changed her mind and closed it again. She didn't say much for the remainder of the lunch-break, and she walked home by herself instead of with Julia. The next day she acted like she'd never even heard of Kenzo.

'Hey, listen up,' she said. 'I met this guy, Damian, last night, on a chat line. He's eighteen and he works for IBM in Melbourne. I saw his picture on his website and everything. He looks like Noel Gallagher, only healthier. He's like, a total honey.'

'Dear Lord, thank you for the internet,' said Lisa, and we went on to discuss what we were going to wear to the Save the Forest Rally on Saturday.

SEVEN: Mrs Dempster told us that she used to work for Apple Records when she was eighteen. She reckoned she knew The Beatles. Yeah, really, I thought, but the next time she went home to water her plants she brought us a photograph of her sitting on a sofa with John, Ringo, George and Paul. Her hair was dyed blue-black and she wore a black and white op-art mini-dress and white leather boots.

'How goddamn frigging amazing,' said Bing.

'Bing!' said Josh.

'It's cool,' said Mrs D.

EIGHT: I made a peepshow.

HOW TO MAKE A PEEPSHOW

Find a shoe box. Take off the lid. Make tiny people from
matchsticks and cotton, or with wire and fabric. Give them
colourful woollen hair. Draw faces: sparkling eyes, rosy cheeks,
forever smiles. Trim fabric scraps for rugs, make furniture
from matchboxes. Put in a tiny pink plastic baby, tucked in
a matchbox cradle, with a cotton wool mattress and a
scrap of soft cloth for a quilt. Glue pictures on the walls,
or a little mirror made with shiny foil. Add a vase of flowers.
Tiny blossoms from your garden, or tissue paper flowers.
Hang a sun or a moon from the box lid. Put the lid on.
Now cut a hole in the end of the box and look inside.

talking to turtles

Bing liked Mrs D right from the start, and as time went on
Josh seemed to accept her as well. I didn't. On the surface
she was friendly to me but I didn't trust her. I was polite to
her but I kept out of her way as much as possible. There was
a coolness between us and that was that.

The first week melted into the second.

Minutes became hours and afternoons became evenings.

Time passed. Or did it?

Perhaps time stays still and it is human beings who do the
moving?

This was the amazingly profound idea that drifted into my head as I lazed around in the garden one afternoon, deep in the depths of last summer. It was scary. I never had big cosmic thoughts. I decided not to talk to Josh about it as he loved nothing better than to discuss physics with me, and I couldn't actually understand much of what he was on about. We don't have the same sort of brain.

Here's an example of a typical me-and-Josh physics discussion. 'Bec, get this.' Josh sticks his tousled head up out of his science magazine. 'It's a fascinating article about Dawkin's latest theory. He has discovered that all matter can be broken down into barcodes. Isn't that amazing? Absolutely everything consists of barcodes.'

'Stephen Hawkins?' I say.

'Bec! Not him, Dawkins.'

Josh looks pained and goes back to reading his whizz-bang magazine.

I'm a great disappointment to him as far as physics is concerned. I can't even remember the names of his favourite physicists, let alone tell a quark from a black hole. Barcodes, I was thinking. Barcodes? How could a butterfly with turquoise and gold speckled wings consist of barcodes? Blackberry pie with thick cream, barcodes? I didn't get it. Furthermore, how can so many abstract theories fit into one small boy's brain, and be so wildly exciting to the owner of that brain, while so few of them will fit into the brain of his somewhat intelligent older sister? People are so different and life is a mystery, that's all I can say. Wow, more profound thoughts. This was getting really scary.

It was beautiful, sitting in the garden. It was the time of day when everything lights up and then vanishes into the dusk. A flock of white cockatoos were spread out on the lawn, pecking away at seeds. One by one they flew up into the branches of the gum tree, squawking raucously at each other as if the world, and not just the day, was coming to an end.

'Don't worry, Theodore.' Bing came around the corner with her turtle in the palm of her hand. She hadn't seen me yet. 'I'll look after you. Cockatoos don't eat turtles, well I don't think they do. Hello, Bec, what are you doing?'

'Nothing really, Bingo. I'm just sitting here having amazingly brilliant thoughts, and watching the cockies. How about you?'

'I'm taking Theodore for a walk. Mrs D said I couldn't watch any more television, and Begonia is asleep. She's had a very busy day.'

'Begonia, or Mrs D?'

'Don't be silly, Bec. Begonia, of course. I gave her some dried apricot to eat and she went all manic and frolicked around like a nutter. Actually Mrs D is in a very bad mood.'

'Oh?'

'Yeah, she growled at Josh big-time because she found

three smelly old sandwiches in his schoolbag, sometimes he forgets to eat them, and she was crotchety with me about turning off the television. She said it crossly instead of nicely. Yeah,' Bing went on. 'Mrs D is okay but I'm missing Vera and Lewis a bit. I hope Vera remembers my sea monkeys.'

Bing sat down beside me. I put my arm around her and ruffled her wonky hair. It felt nice. 'I miss them too, Bingo,' I told her, but then I couldn't think what else to say about it so we talked animal stuff instead. We came to the conclusion that cockatoos do eat turtles, but that if turtles tucked their heads and legs in very fast and kept them tucked away for ages they would be safe. Bing was worried because turtles don't exactly have a reputation for speed, but I told her that if turtles were that hopeless they'd have been extinct long ago.

Big sisters are important. Part of their job is to be reassuring and cheery. I don't get the opportunity to be a big sister very often because Bing is such a know-it-all and very independent. Pretending to be an authority on wildlife made me feel a whole lot better about being such a fizz at physics, but I wished I knew the cure for missing someone.

~~~

When it got dark we went in for dinner. The house smelled awful. It turned out Mrs D had a migraine coming on, and she had burnt the chicken curry. It was still edible though, if you mixed it up with plenty of rice and a big dollop of the yoghurt and coriander goo.

'Yummy goo,' I said, to make Mrs D feel better about the burnt curry.

'It's a raita, actually, Bec. Raita are served with curries, they're small side dishes that have special flavours and textures to complement the main dish.'

Silly old cow! On one hand she sneered at us for being foodies and then she had to go and embarrass me with a lecture about Indian cuisine, just when I was making an effort to be nice to her.

'Anyhow, kids, I'm off to bed,' Dorky Doreen continued. 'It's the only thing I can do when I get a headache from hell like this. Don't stay up too late, will you?'

'We won't,' we promised sweetly, and played Monopoly until midnight. Josh scored all the stations but Bing won because she cunningly put hotels on Park Lane and Mayfair. We watched a bit of *Rage* but it was really boring so we ate big bowls of butter-pecan ice-cream and went to bed.

I lay under my quilt, thinking about missing. Missing is strange. Sometimes it isn't there at all, and then it swoops and knocks you flat. It hurts in your guts and in your hollow heart and you want to cry but you don't, because there's no point. The people you are missing have gone away, and you are alone, and the night is very large and very dark.

postcards from america

The first postcard was from Lewis and Vera. It was a picture of a neon-pink convertible painted with day-glo flowers, on a bright green background. Six crazy cats were riding along in the crazy car. They were wearing cowboy hats and playing assorted instruments with crazy-cat abandon.

San Francisco is fabulous. The Lotus Hotel has big white
fluffy everything, a phone and a TV in the bathroom,
and a great view of the bay. A huge crowd came to the
book signing at Barnes and Noble, and we were feted with
champagne and lobster at Chez Panisse by the publishers.
I miss my three beautiful darlings so much. xoxo love
from Mum. Hello, you three. So this is America!
Some wonderful buildings in this vibrant city. I love the
Latino food and the murals in the Mission district, but it's
very sad and challenging to witness so many homeless
people in the streets. Sending you blessings every day.
All my love, Dad.

The second postcard was from my best buddy Eloise in New York. It was a photograph of an exquisite papery pink poppy floating in white space.

hey Bec, new york is so cool now that i am getting the hang
of it. on saturday i went to a free concert in central park and

i saw Blink 182. it was joy, they really rocked. i have an
after-school job in an organic grocery store and am really
into skateboarding now. you should see me ollie. i miss you
big-time. write to me at once. luv luv luv from eloise.

San Francisco. New York. Suddenly my life felt incredibly
tedious. School, home, homework, TV. School, home, homework, TV. Repeat until you die of boredom. The biggest thrill
of my week was cleaning my flute valves and getting eighty-
three percent in my French vocab test. Whoopdy-doo. I read
the postcards twice then mooched around eating crackers
with butter and Vegemite for a while, feeling sorry for myself,
but no one even noticed. Mrs D was busy on the phone,
talking to the woman at the kennel because Elmore the
Second had an abscess on his leg. Josh was down at Mr
Patrick's place as usual, and Bing and Begonia were glued to
the screen watching the stupid afternoon kids' shows. Some
doofus dressed up as a cuddly bear was dancing through a
forest of fake trees, playing a recorder. Come to think of it, I
hadn't cleaned my flute valves for ages because I didn't have
any acid-free paper. You can only buy it at a music shop but
you can use cigarette paper instead, if you remove the gluey
bit. I didn't have any cigarette papers either so I thought I'd
go and get some at the deli. A bike ride might be a good
idea. Anything would be better than doing my homework.
There's only so much enthusiasm one can feel for an essay

about the dramatic construction of *King Lear*. It would have been different if Eloise were here. We'd have hung out and done our essays together. I grabbed a flowery note-card, an airmail sticker and a couple of stamps from Vera's study.

Dear Lady Eloise, I have been locked in the black tower by a nasty evil witch. The days are dark and lonely, and a rat is nibbling at my toes. Please harness the dragon with haste, and travel the blue and gold cloud realms to rescue me. From your beloved Maid Bec.

'Bing, I'm going to the shops. I'll be back by dinnertime. Tell Mrs D, okay?'

'Sure,' said Bing vaguely. I bet she wouldn't remember. Too bad.

'Bring me some lollies,' she added. I wouldn't. Too bad.

I cycled as fast as I could, past the orange orchard, past Mr Patrick's place, down the hill, past the vineyard, past the huge brick mansion with two lion statues on the fake-pillar gate posts. No one ever seemed to be home at that house. Josh reckoned it belonged to a drug baron. An accountant with dodgy taste, more likely. Turn right at Orchard Road, past the leafy hedges of the posh houses, left at the lights, and straight on for five blocks. Welcome to urban sprawlsville. Jamieson Avenue is a boring road thick with businesses that have big ugly signs, like instant printing places and pool-care equipment shops. It's a road where you have to concentrate hard, because there's heaps of traffic. I sped along on the pavement instead. There were never any cops around.

The shops nearest to us are basic: a video store, a deli, a newsagent, and a hairdresser-cum-beauty salon where Vera says no one with any sense would ever go, mainly because she went there once for a leg wax and came home with red spotted legs covered with brown waxy gunk. I bought a packet of Zig Zag papers at the deli, hoping Mrs Cheng behind the counter didn't think I was going to use them to smoke whacky weed. I considered telling her it was for cleaning my flute valves but decided that it sounded like a cover up. 'Never complain, never explain,' I said to myself, pretending I was an elegant jazz singer with a mysterious past.

I hung out in the newsagent for a while, so I could have a rest before riding home. The guy behind the counter didn't seem to mind if people looked through the magazines and then didn't buy them. He never said anything, anyhow. I looked up my horoscope in *Woman's Day*. I love Athena Starwoman. Lisa says that astrologers just make stuff up, and make it so broad that it could apply to anyone. I wasn't so sure. Whenever I read Athena her predictions seemed to fit my week perfectly. Lisa reckons I only believe it because I'm gullible, but I reckon she thinks that because she's a Scorpio. Scorpios can be very cynical.

~~~

LEO: The moon in Jupiter will bring you some unexpected good luck this week. Your finances are about to take a lucky turn. Think carefully, however, before making any major decisions as Mars in Leo will make for a certain amount of turbulence. Lucky number: two. Lucky colour: apricot.

The man behind the counter gave a gentle cough. I wasn't sure if it was real coughing, or if he was doing it to indicate that he was annoyed with me for reading the magazines. Maybe I should buy something, so I wouldn't look such a user. I was thinking about what Lisa said. If all the horoscopes were totally general, then how could Athena say that Leos were going to get lucky with money this week and get away with it. It would be too much of a coincidence if a twelfth of the population suddenly got lucky with money, but surely no one would read her if what she said never came true? Well, that was all very interesting but it was time I got going. I put the *Woman's Day* back neatly. The guy behind the counter was staring at me, so I decided to buy a Kit Kat. I could eat half of it and give the rest to Bing.

As I handed over the money I smiled innocently at him. He smiled back. Sometimes it helps to be an ordinary-looking girl. I bet if I had dreads and a lip stud he wouldn't be so smiley. Out of the blue I had a flash of inspiration. I would buy a two-dollar Scratch Lotto ticket. Athena said my lucky number was two. If I won something it would prove that Athena really was a Magic Star Goddess. I would have to win at least twenty dollars though, or Lisa wouldn't be convinced. Josh and Bing and I sometimes bought dollar scratchies with our pocket money on Saturday mornings. We never won more than a couple of bucks. The whole thrill of it was the moment of possibility when you got your five-cent coin and gently scratched the silvery layers off to see what was underneath. Just for a moment a thousand, ten thousand dollars were yours. Until they weren't. 'A dollar's worth of dreams,' Lewis called it.

I carefully scratched my ticket. The first number I uncovered was five hundred dollars. Two dollars came up next. Then ten thousand. Damn. I already knew I wasn't going to win anything. I scratched a fourth box and saw another five hundred dollars. Yeah, well. Been there, done that. You usually got two of some numbers to trick you into believing you might get three. They did that to keep your hopes up so you'd believe you had almost won that time, and buy more tickets. It was such a scam.

I knew exactly what was going to happen before it even did. The next number that came up would be some unbelievable amount like twenty thousand or a thousand or something, and the last one would be two dollars again. I could already feel the small pang of disappointment that comes with not winning. I scratched for the fifth time. Yup, I was right. Twenty thousand. I scratched the last tiny square off. Two dollars. No good. Chuck it in the bin. Hey, wait a minute. It wasn't two dollars. It was five hundred. I looked again. Five hundred! Slowly I counted again. There was no mistaking it. There were three five hundreds. I had won five hundred dollars.

I handed my scratchy to the man. I expected him to say that there was a mistake, but he took the card, examined it, and smiled at me.

'It's your lucky day, sweetheart.' He opened the till, counted out some notes, and casually handed me the money. Five crisp green hundred dollar notes. I was only used to blue pocket-money tens and orange Christmas-money twenties. The green hundreds didn't look real, they looked like play money.

'Here you go,' said the man. He handed me a packet of gold-wrapped toffees as well. 'Congratulations!'

'Wow,' I said. 'I didn't realise I would get the money, like, right away.'

'Actually five hundred dollars is the most I can pay out. If you win more you have to go in and collect it from the Lotteries Commission. Beaut job, that, I reckon, handing over the money to the big winners.'

'For sure,' I replied. 'Thank you. Um, bye.'

lucky stars

It was the best feeling. Cycling home on a summery afternoon, chewing on a crunchy chocolate Kit Kat, carrying a packet of cigarette papers, a bag of toffees and five hundred dollars; a heap of lovely money that fell from the sky by magic and was mine to spend on whatever I wanted. An hour ago everything was totally rank and now it was totally brilliant. The sky was turning a dusky amber, and the big crimson hollyhocks in Mr Patrick's yard glowed like glorious joyous beacons.

I was just in time. Mrs D was dishing out the dinner. I plonked the packet of toffees down on the bench and sat down at the table.

'Yay, lollies!' Bing grinned at me with delight.

'Smells good, Mrs D, what are we having?' I asked.

'Salmon loaf and greek salad. Nothing heavy. We have to save lots of room for dessert. I made lemon delicious pudding, it's my favourite. I got a craving for it today.'

'Superb,' I answered.

'You seem remarkably cheerful, Bec. What's up?'

'Nothing. Yummoh, this tastes great.'

Even Mrs D was my friend that night. Life was a bowl of cherries. I didn't tell anyone about the win, though. It was my secret.

~~~

The next day was Saturday. I caught the bus to town to meet my friends at the Forest Rally. I wore a moss-green top, my apricot chiffon skirt, and my one-and-only piece of real jewellery, the green glass necklace that used to belong to my grandmother. I thought I looked rather fine. Even my hair did what it was supposed to for once.

The rally was good. There were lots of people there: older straight-looking people, ferals with dreads, families with babies in pushers, kids like us. Organisers dressed as koalas were rattling donation tins and getting petitions signed. We hung around for a while, sprawled on the grass under the trees, listening to the reggae band and the stirring speeches.

'The trouble with this is, the people who are here believe this stuff anyhow,' Lisa said.

'Yeah, I guess,' said Katherine, 'but at least it will get some publicity on TV and in the paper if people make a stink. I mean you have to do *something*, right? You can't just not do anything.'

'I dunno,' said Lisa. 'On the news they show the weirdest people, like that loony-looking guy doing the drumming over there, and make it seem like just a bunch of crazies. And the petitions, well, the pollies probably just stick them in the bin and continue to do the most profitable thing. I think you have to be more radical, like go down to the forest blockade and tie yourself to a tree, actually stop the bulldozers . . .'

'So why don't you?' asked Jaz.

'I'm considering it. At Easter. I know a guy down at the blockade,' replied Lisa.

We all stared at her. Lisa is a mysterious person, a whole lot of contradictions in one body. She has two navel rings and a tiny tattoo of a rose on her ankle. She wears outrageous sexy clothes, black clingy things and tiny halter tops and ultra-short skirts. She might look like a tarty air-head yet she's brilliant at maths and science, and has a sharp analytical mind. Lisa was the only one of us who wasn't a virgin until Katherine bonked Kenzo. She's secretive about the details but I think Lisa has slept with quite a few guys. She has a dry sense of humour and she can be bitchy sometimes, hard and nasty right out of the blue.

'Anyhow, I have to cut loose. I have to be at work by three,' Lisa continued. 'Forests come and forests go but people still have to eat burgers, right?'

'Yeah, we'd better go too. Katherine and I are going to Eros to pick up the dress I've got on lay-by. Wait till you see it, it's stunning,' said Julia.

Jaz and I watched Julia and Katherine disappearing across the park. They are a very unlikely looking pair of friends. Julia is tall and slender, with short black hair and pale skin. She is such a style queen. Everything always matches, on Julia. That day she was wearing a black and white fifties dress, strappy black sandals and silvery nail polish. Her fringe was pinned back with a sparkly flower clip. Katherine is tall, too, but she is large and lumpy with it. Her face is plump and friendly and her long auburn hair tends to frizz up and fly all over the place. Katherine loves to wear the latest things but somehow she puts them together all wrong. In her Stussy t-shirt, Nike trainers, Levi jeans and Arnette sunnies she stomped across the field, talking away happily, while Julia wafted elegantly along beside her.

'Whatcha doing tonight, Bec?' asked Jaz.

'Nothing, really. Might look around the shops for a while, then go home.'

'Want to come over and stay the night at my place? My mother won't mind. Actually I think my parents are going out . . . we could get some videos or something.'

'Yeah, sure. I'll have to ring Mrs D but it should be no problem.'

'Great. Let's go window shopping then. Want to go to Dada records?' said Jaz.

~~~~

I love Dada records. You go down a narrow flight of stairs and suddenly you're in a dark cave, a world of music. All the staff look totally cool and funky, and the shop stocks the latest CDs plus heaps of hard-to-get second-hand stuff.

'Hey, Jaz, look, here's the Tea Party album, the one that's got my favourite song on it. It's only fifteen bucks, that's pretty good.'

'Gonna get it?'

I opened my mouth to say 'Nah, can't afford it', and then I remembered. I could buy twenty CDs if I wanted to.

'Yeah, for sure. I just love that song, you know, *The River*, it's the best,' I told Jaz.

'Hey, that's weird,' she replied. 'My brother loves that song too. I've gone off it now because he plays it over and over.' Jaz wandered off to check out the posters, or maybe she was checking out the guy who was checking out the posters. He was gorgeous. He had dark curly hair and he looked intelligent. Handsome guys who wear glasses always do. I was glad Jaz was over the other side of the shop because I didn't want her to notice the hundred dollar bill I handed to the tongue-studded girl behind the counter. Jaz would be sure to ask how come I had a hundred bucks. Maybe I would tell her my secret, but not right now. I wanted it for myself, as bright and cheery as a yellow daisy, for a little while longer.

After Dada, Jaz and I bought a drink and some hot chips, and sat in Forest Place. The day was sunny; the sky was huge and blue. It felt great to hang out with my friend and not have to be anywhere or do anything in particular.

'I didn't know you had a brother,' I said to Jaz, as I sculled my apple juice.

'I've got two. Tan is the oldest, he's twenty-four. He just finished his PhD at Monash. Tan is kind of a computer genius. Nick, the one who likes Tea Party, is seventeen. He's just started Landscape Architecture at Uni. You might meet him at my house, although he might not come home. You never know with Nick.'

yummy fizzy whizzy wonderful

We headed for the station to catch the train to Jaz's place. The shortest route was to cut through Myers. The cosmetic department was packed with shoppers in search of eternal youth serum at a hundred dollars a jar. Jaz and I ignored the snooty gazes of the sales staff and sprayed ourselves with the most expensive perfumes we could find. I chose Joy and Jaz chose Beautiful. We smelled like princesses, like lightness and clouds and laughter. After the cosmetics counters we hit the section by the escalator, with all the groovy goods and girlie stuff. I love gorgeous goodies like that but usually I just browse because of the mega-fierce prices. That afternoon was different. Now I was a rich girl whose parents were a million miles away. I could do what I liked. I was no longer sensible Bec. I was daring and dangerous. I was Xena Warrior Woman meets the Girlie Goddess.

I bought:

Three bath bombs: tangerine, lavender, and honeysuckle
A big tub of vanilla almond body goo
A bar of transparent purple soap dappled with violet petals
A tiny blue glass bottle of jasmine-rose floral body splash
for Jaz

A brown bear soap for Bing and a turquoise seahorse soap
for Josh
A cucumber and seaweed face masque for Mrs D
And get this. I bought a packet of dark-red henna.

'Shall I?' I asked Jaz.

'Sure, why not? Red is the ultimate. I'll help you do it tonight
if you like.'

~~~~

The train was crowded but we grabbed a seat.

'Hey, Bec,' Jaz asked as the train sped along. 'How come
you're on such a spendathon?'

It was the moment of truth. I could have fudged it and
made up a story about Christmas present money or something but I decided to tell her.

'That's so wild,' she said. 'Man, five hundred bucks! What
are you going to do with the rest of the money?'

'I don't know.' I thought about it. 'I suppose I could put it
in the bank. That feels really boring but I don't want to fritter
it away on little things. I mean, my spend-up was fun and all,
but I'd like to do something major. I don't know what yet
though.

'Cool,' said Jaz.

That was what I liked about Jaz now that I was getting
to know her better. She had a sort of acceptingness about
her. Katherine would have come up with a hundred and one

suggestions about label brands that she thought were hot, Julia would have hinted that I should buy her something, and Lisa would have said something dry and bizarre, like 'let's have a drug binge', but Jaz just smiled and said 'Cool'.

We got off the train in Mt Lawley, a posh suburb not far from the city, and wandered down the leafy streets. Most of the houses are gracious old mansions but Jaz's house was white and ultra-modern. The velvety green lawn was edged with pale pink roses in terracotta pots. Each rose bush had been trained into an elegant ball shape.

'You never told me you were a millionaire,' I blurted.

'We're only renting,' Jaz replied.

For a minute I wondered if I'd said the wrong thing, or if I had imagined a touch of coolness in her reply.

'Yeah, but still. What a palace.'

'Mmm,' mumbled Jaz, as she scrabbled for her door key.

The kitchen was sleek and minimal, all white and gleaming, like something out of a glossy lifestyle magazine. Even the mangoes and capsicums on the square glass platter were beautifully arranged. How come they had so many mangoes? Maybe they were into smoothies. Propped up against a red vase containing white lilies was a piece of paper.

Jaz glanced at the note. 'Yep, we've got the house to ourselves. My parents have gone to a cocktail party, and then a business dinner. They won't be home until really late.'

'What does your father do?' I asked. Even though we had

been hanging out at school for a few weeks now I realised there was heaps I didn't know about Jaz.

'Real estate. My mother, too.'

'They must be really good at it.'

There was a silence.

'Actually, not so much,' said Jaz. 'I might as well tell you. My parents are, well, how can I explain it . . . let's say my parents are high-flyers but they aren't always that lucky. Sometimes we have heaps of money, sometimes we have none. When things are going well we have the best of everything but sometimes it gets kind of tricky. Like, I'm pretty sure they left a few debts behind in Malaysia. They're always on to some new fantastic scheme or get-rich plan, always full of promises about the next best thing. Sometimes it really gets to me.'

'Oh,' I said. 'That must be tough.' It felt like a dumb comment but I couldn't think of a better one.

'Yeah, it's life though, isn't it? Love them or hate them, you can't do much about your parents. Let's go up to my bedroom. You want something to eat?'

'Nah, maybe later.'

~~~~

Jaz's bedroom was stunning. On one wall was a corkboard covered with postcards and photographs and cartoons and feathers and sparkly bits of broken jewellery. There were six tiny troll dolls with electric rainbow hair pinned next to a

Barbie doll with a missing leg and a shaved head.

The bed was a futon with a white cover. Beside the bed was a chunky white candle and a heap of books and magazines. Jaz's clothes hung in the corner on a bamboo rack. She didn't have many clothes, but she did have plenty of hats. There was a maroon velvet hat with a black rose on it, a funny old straw sun hat, a beret, and a Mambo cap. Jaz even had her own verandah, with two white cane chairs and a white cane coffee table. On the table was a tiny bent bonsai tree in a glazed pot. There was a joy view of tree-tops and gardens.

'Great verandah. Great view. Great hats,' I said.

'Yeah, I love hats, even though I am mainly too shy to wear them.'

'You don't seem shy, Jaz. I mean your red hair and everything . . .'

'Must be just a good actress, maybe. I think everyone is shy, inside. We just cover it up in different ways. Anyhow, that reminds me. Do you want to henna your hair today or not? If so, let's bung it on now because it has to stay on your hair for ages.'

'Yeah, why not,' I replied. 'First I should ring Mrs D, and then let's do it, before I pike out.'

HOW TO HENNA YOUR HAIR

If you want to colour your hair, henna is really good because commercial hair dyes wreck your hair. They also cost heaps, and some of the weird chemicals used in them have been found to cause cancer. Henna is all natural, in fact it's a type of mud found in Persia and India, and it makes your hair strong and shiny, as well as a fabulous new colour. First buy your henna, in a health food shop or a trendy place like Lush or The Body Shop. It doesn't cost much. There are heaps of colours: black, brown, gold and various reds. Pick a shade. Take the packet home. Even though it's a strange funny-coloured powder, you have to trust it. Stash it until you have a day at home by yourself, or until you live with sympathetic people who won't laugh and call you a dag.

Dyeing your hair with henna is messy. Put on old clothes. Put the henna in a glass bowl. Add boiling water, and stir until you have a nice mucky goop the consistency of thick custard. Keep going until there are no lumps, or at least no major ones. Get some plastic wrap, an old towel, a shower cap, and an old dark coloured face-cloth, or a rag. Unless you want stained fingers, put on rubber gloves. Wet your hair and carefully apply the warm mud to your head. Dollops will fall on the floor and the hand basin but never mind. Use the old face cloth to wipe them up, and to remove the smudges from your cheeks and hairline. Start at the top of your head and continue until all your hair is covered with henna paste, then wrap your head in plastic film, and put on the shower cap. The towel goes over your shoulders in case little bits fall down, which they will. Now read a book, bake a cake, or sit in the garden and daydream. After three hours go into the shower and wash the mud from your head. At first it will be messy and mucky brown goop will splodge all over the shower stall but soon it will wash away. When the water rinses clear come out of the shower. Put on your finest clothes. Dry your hair. Look in the mirror. You are a divine and radiant creature. But do not leave messy blobs all over the bathroom or the henna will stain the porcelain and your parents will kill you.

oh no

I washed my hair in the elegant bathroom. I put on my knickers and Jaz lent me her oldest t-shirt. I looked at the towels dubiously. They were white and fluffy, just like in a posh hotel, so Jaz found a brown bath mat for me in a cupboard. I put the bath mat around my shoulders, and then we did it, the henna thing. When my hair was wrapped in Clingwrap I looked completely silly.

'Three hours,' said Jaz. 'Come on, let's get some food and watch TV. If there's nothing on I've got some *Friends* tapes we can watch.'

Here's what we found in the fridge: shiraz and mineral water, a tub of butter, a carton of eggs, the remains of a pot of pâté, some bean shoots, and various take-away containers of food that no longer looked very appetising.

'My mother is very bright,' said Jaz. 'However, she isn't what you'd call a practical woman. She buys ten mangoes because they look stylish, even though none of us like them much, but she forgets to buy milk. My father is even worse. He thinks whisky counts as food. Actually, we eat out a lot.'

We found some crackers and put them on a plate with the pâté. '*Voila*, a lovely bean sprout garnish!' Jaz exclaimed. I think she was sort of embarrassed but I didn't care about the lack of food. It was just neat to be hanging out at her house with no adults around. I was panicking a bit about my hair though, hoping that it would come out a nice shade of dark red and not weirdly orange or something. Jaz and I sat on the couch and watched *Friends* for a while. I like Phoebe the best.

After we'd scoffed the pâté Jaz said, 'I'm starving', so we foraged around in the kitchen again. The pantry wasn't exactly a treasure trove of incredible edibles either. We found stuff that you couldn't actually call dinner, like jars of olives and designer chutney, and a loaf of rather stale bread.

'I could make scrambled eggs,' I said. 'This bread would make good toast. Do you have any parsley?'

'I dunno . . . maybe . . . I know we have some ornamental rosemary bushes. I'll go check it out.'

I couldn't find a frying pan but there was a wok in the cupboard so I got started. I cracked six eggs in a bowl, beat them until they were fluffy, and poured the mixture into the wok on top of a big knob of sizzling butter. I put four slices of bread in the gleaming silver toaster. Timing is the thing with scrambled eggs. One minute they're a gooey liquid. The next minute they're creamy and delicious but if you don't take them off the heat at exactly the right moment they suddenly turn into a rubbery disaster.

'This is ready. Where are you? I need parsley. I need salt,' I yelled.

'I'm right here and there should be some salt around somewhere or at least some soya sauce . . . as for parsley, I don't like your chances. Whatever it is smells superb, though,' came the reply.

What was going on? The voice came from the wrong place. Jaz had gone out the back and this voice came from the entrance hall. Not only that, it was the wrong voice. I turned around. There was a guy standing in the kitchen smiling at me. He looked a lot like Jaz, only taller, and his hair wasn't postbox red, it was black. He wore faded blue jeans and a white t-shirt with a Tin Tin cartoon on it.

'I'm Nick,' he said. 'Who are you?'

No wonder he was smiling. There was a total stranger, dressed in white cotton undies and a saggy grey t-shirt, with cling-wrapped mud all over her head, in his kitchen, doing something weird in a wok, yelling commands at the top of her voice. I looked a complete wally. I wished I could vanish, but there was no place to run and no place to hide. I had to brazen it out.

'I'm Bec, Jaz's friend. She's out the back looking for parsley. Want some scrambled eggs?' My voice came out quite normally. What a miracle.

'Yeah, if there's enough,' said Nick. Just then, Jaz returned, clutching a small bouquet of parsley.

'Hey, Nick,' she said, as if nothing extraordinary was happening. It was no big deal for her, seeing as he was her brother and she had proper clothes on.

'I found some parsley. We don't have any in our garden, the lady next door gave me this. Nick, this is Bec. She's staying the night.'

'Cool,' said Nick.

I concentrated on throwing some more eggs into the wok, and buttering the toast.

The classic thing was, it turned out to be the best night. While Nick was putting some music on I made a panic face at Jaz, and she fetched her kimono for me to wear. It was gorgeous blue silk with red chrysanthemums.

'What if I get goop on it?'

'You won't. The henna is almost dry now, mud woman.'

I pretended I was a movie star drifting around in my exotic robe, which helped me forget that I looked an utter doofus.

The scrambled eggs were a bit strange but on buttery toast they tasted fine. Nick got out a really bizarre video about a girl who morphs into a supernatural butterfly woman and saves the planet from the forces of evil. He brought a tub of triple-chocolate ice-cream as well, and the three of us lounged around eating it straight from the tub and making silly comments about the movie.

When it was over, my big moment arrived. There was a dreadful mess in the shower at first, all rusty red as though there had been a bloody murder, but I shoved the gunk down the drain hole with my foot and rinsed for ages until the water ran clear. I bunged on almond conditioner, ran the comb through the knots, rinsed again, blow-dried my hair, and guess what? It was dark plum red, and gorgeous and shiny, even better than I had hoped. Utter doofus morphs into Radiant Red Goddess. Now I am Bec the Magnificent, Queen of the Night.

Jaz was lying on her back on the couch waving her feet in the air. 'You look brilliant, Bec. Welcome to the wonderful world of wild red-haired women. Nick went to bed,' she said. 'Hey, why don't we crash too? I'm pooped.'

I was given the guest room next door to Jaz. It had pink walls, pale green carpet, and crisp linen patterned with roses. I even had a pink bathroom and my own double bed. I fell asleep in no time at all, into a place deeper than dreaming.

When I woke up in the morning I didn't know what time

it was. It felt kind of late but I wasn't sure. I decided to get up anyhow. I dressed in my apricot skirt and green top and I looked at myself in the mirror. My green glass necklace sparkled and shone and wow, I thought, look at my new red hair!

I tip-toed down the hall and peeked into Jaz's room. She was sound asleep. I felt funny about waking her up. I didn't know what else to do, so I went back and sat on my bed. I was hungry. The scrambled eggs and ice-cream seemed a long time ago.

'Good morning.' It was Nick, standing in my doorway. This time he was wearing black cargo pants and a black t-shirt with a picture of Bob Marley on it. 'No one gets up early in this house except me. And you. Do you want some breakfast?'

Nick and I sat in the sunny courtyard outside the kitchen. We ate toast with pâté, and mangoes. I cut the mangoes Vera's way—you make big slices down each side, score the flesh, and turn the skin back so you have beautiful square bits of juicy mango just ready to bite off.

'Good one,' said Nick. 'If you eat them the other way you get stringy bits in your teeth.'

He smiled at me, a wide generous smile. Nick's face was open and friendly. In fact, he was absolutely drop-dead gorgeous: tall, with jet-black hair cut short and snazzy, and smooth skin the colour of milky coffee. Nick was very easy to be with, just like Jaz. He told me all about his Landscape

Architecture course, which sounded great. He'd just designed a mirrored screen for a furniture assignment and his next project was to design and create a garden with a specific theme.

'I might do a Zen one, very simple with rocks and gravel, or else a really bizarre one, with sculptures made of the debris of our culture. I haven't decided yet, but I've lined up a friend of my father's who wants a garden area designed. He's a pretty okay guy, so that should be sweet.'

I told Nick about Vera being a famous cook, and what had happened to my father, and that my parents were travelling in America. 'I miss them, but they'll be home in three weeks. The time is going really quickly.'

Jaz appeared, sleepily, and made a pot of Earl Grey tea. All of a sudden, I felt shy. Nick and Jaz weren't saying much, and I couldn't think of anything to say either.

'I'd better split, Jaz,' I said, gulping down my tea. 'I told Mrs D I'd be home in the morning.'

'I'll walk you to the station,' said Jaz.

'See ya, Bec,' said Nick. He smiled at me, that gorgeous smile again, and headed upstairs.

~~~

'So, how do you like my brother?' Jaz asked as we strolled along. She looked fresh and funky in baggy black shorts and a white t-shirt, with her hair gelled up in cute little peaks on top of her head. With Jaz and Nick all my stereotypes about Asian people were being challenged. It was kind of like they stepped out of their culture and into ours, and did it to the max, even better than we did. Jaz and Nick were utterly cool. They could have stepped straight out of an Esprit ad, a world of perfectly groovy people. I suddenly felt silly and old fashioned in my boring skirt and top.

'Nick . . . he's nice.'

'Yeah,' said Jaz. 'Everybody likes Nick. In Malaysia all the girls had the hots for him but he never went out with anyone for very long. My parents worry about him. They think he's gay or something.'

'Is he?'

'I don't think so. He's just into his music, and his Uni work, and skateboarding and stuff. Nick is just Nick. He hates being tied down to anything.'

'I can understand that. As for guys, I'm not really interested in them, especially the dorky ones at our school. Are you?'

'Back home in Kuala Lumpur there was a boy and he was my friend. His name was Bennett. We used to go places together but he never tried to kiss me or anything. My mother thought he might be gay as well, but that's probably just my mother. Hey, let's run, I can hear the train.'

I got my ticket just in time.

As the train took off Jaz made silly finger signals at me, jumping up and down and waving her arms like a loony. She was such fun and it had been a brilliant night. Suddenly I felt very flat, probably because I had to go home and do my homework, and then it would be Monday morning again.

Life sucks and this is why. The week crawls by like a snail on Valium, you spend most of your time looking forward to the weekend but the sweeter it tastes the quicker it vanishes. I had the Sunday blues. It's a common sickness. Mildly infectious, dreary but not lethal.

I like trains. I like looking out the window into backyards, watching the world whiz past. You see interesting things: a flash of vibrant crimson bougainvillea, a lemon tree, a rusty bicycle propped against a veranda, huge baggy bloomers blatting about on a saggy clothes line. Other people's stuff, other people's lives, to glimpse, just for a moment or two.

However, that day even the train journey didn't lift my spirits. Steady Bec, the sensible girl who looked after her brother and sister and always did her homework, had been replaced by someone else. Bec The Uncertain. Bec Who Does Not Know.

I was a totally muddled mixture of happy and sad, hopeful and devastated. It wasn't just the Sunday blues. I suddenly knew that I really liked Nick, and that there was no way anything would ever come of it. He had no interest in girls, even gorgeous Malaysian ones. I would probably never even see him again. I remembered his slender brown hands and his wide smile. I was somewhere I had never been before. Don't be silly, Bec. You can't have fallen in love.

back at the ranch

The train pulled up just in time for me to hop straight off and connect with the bus to the hills, which was cool. When I got home Mrs D was waving frantically from the window.

'Ooh, look at your lovely hair. Perfect timing, Bec, your parents are on the phone, they're in New York.'

Josh was nowhere to be seen and Bing was sitting on the floor cross-legged, jabbering into the phone and beaming like mad. 'Oh wow, two packets, cool. Yeah, okay, yes, Mum, I will, no worries, Mum, here's Bec, see ya, Mum.'

'How are you, darling?' asked Vera, and then carried straight on without waiting for my reply. 'New York is fabulous, Bec, you would just *adore* it. Our hotel is right next to Eli's, which has to be the best delicatessen in the whole world. They have every kind of bread from poppy seed bagels to organic sour-dough to walnut rye, and the soups, oh my goodness, as for the range of cheeses, you can't imagine, it's just heavenly. Tomorrow we're having lunch with Eloise and her mother, if I can drag your father out of the Museum of Modern Art, that is . . . Now, how is everything going? Mrs D said things were fine, and Bingy seemed happy . . .'

'Yeah, no worries. Josh is good, we're all good, school's okay, I just spent the night over at Jaz's, and I hennaed my hair, it's—'

'Darling, did you?' Vera butted in enthusiastically. 'I bet it looks stunning. Well, here's your father. I love you, sweet pea.

We'll ring again when we get to New Mexico.'

Talking to Lewis was like sailing in a smooth river after the tumbling whirlwind that was Vera. My mother is so alive with speed and energy that sometimes there doesn't seem quite enough room for me, Bec. Lewis was slower and more restful. He told me about the white curving architecture of the Guggenheim, and the beautiful Moon Viewing Pavilion inside the Museum of Modern Art, and how you can see the whole skyline of Manhattan and the green tree-tops of Central Park from the MoMa roof. He said the street musicians were great, and that he loved New York, and he left me a gap to tell him what colour my hair actually was.

~~~

After I got off the phone things got rather interesting.

'Where's Josh?'

'He's down at Patrick's. I'm just going to fetch him home for lunch, actually. I need the exercise,' said Mrs D.

I was busy hunting in the fridge for something to eat and not finding anything very spectacular so I wasn't listening properly, but as soon as Mrs D had gone Bing grabbed me and plonked me down on the couch.

'Bec, guess what, you'll never believe it!'

'What?' I was chomping on my crispy apple, which was all I could find to eat at such short notice.

'Last night when you were out, Josh was down at the cottage and Mr Patrick brought him home because he had a tummy ache, but it was nothing, he only needed a good poo. Mr Patrick stayed for dinner and they drank sherry and got all thingy. He said we must call him Patrick, and he was calling Mrs D Dawn because she said she never liked the name Doreen. Mr Patrick said Dawn was a lovely name and meant new beginnings. Isn't that frigging amazing?'

'Bing, what do you mean, "all thingy"? And how do you know all this anyhow?'

'You know, "all thingy", like boyfriend and girlfriend, except they're old. I heard them because Josh and I were watching *Xena* in here and we could hear them in the kitchen and Mrs D forgot to make us go to bed because she'd had too much sherry. You could tell she had, and guess what else? Vera has got me two packets of sea monkeys but she said not to be disappointed because it's only shrimp brine, like tiny wee prawns, and not really monkeys at all.'

'Wow.' What a blast. It made sense, sort of, because otherwise why would Mrs D walk down to pick up Josh? She was such a couch potato, she'd never even mentioned the word 'exercise' before, and come to think of it, she had just referred to him as Patrick, not Mr Patrick. I thought about it some more. 'Well, it's up to them, I guess. Are you sure you aren't imagining it, though?'

'No way!' Bing was adamant. 'Josh thought so too. You wait and see, but Bec, I have to make something out of fruit and vegetables for my Health homework. Will you help me?

I don't want to make some dumb little dog sculpture from a carrot and toothpicks. That's what everyone will do. I want to make something really cool.'

'Sure, Bingo. Let's check out the crisper.'

~~~

It was all very strange but it turned out that Bing was right. During lunch Mrs D mentioned, casually, that Patrick was coming up after dinner to teach her to play chess. I say 'casually', but it was that sort of casual that isn't really casual. Love in the Twilight Zone. How bizarre, I thought, but I didn't have a problem with it.

Bing and I had a superb afternoon. I hunted through Lewis's art books until I found what I was looking for, paintings by this Italian guy, Arcimboldo, who worked for the Emperor Rudolph of Prague. He used to make amazing collage heads, like if you were a scholar he would make your portrait from books, or if you were a cook he'd make your picture out of cooking implements. Bing and I glued olives and lentils and carrot slices and stuff on cardboard and created this amazing face. The spinach leaf hair with the orange-peel bow looked particularly spectacular. Madame Jardin, we called her.

I went upstairs to think about doing my dreaded Human Biology assignment and noticed Josh sitting at his desk looking very forlorn.

'Hey, Josh.'

'Hey.'

'What's up?'

'Nothing.'

He was doodling a scrawl of black inky sketches of dark faces and spooky creatures.

'Come on, Josh Bosh, now what's the matter?'

'Nothing.'

'Bing told me about last night, about Mr Patrick and Mrs D. Is that what's bothering you?'

'Yeah, well . . . it's just that Mr Patrick is *my* friend, and I don't have many friends, and now if he's going to be . . . you know, keen on Mrs D, well, it changes things. It's like, everyone's got somebody. Bing has Megan and Begonia and Theodore and you've got lots of friends, but I only have Mr Patrick.'

I thought about it for a while. Josh is special, and he deserved something better than a slick response. I didn't know what to say but I had to say something. I took a deep breath. 'Everybody feels lonely sometimes,' I said.

'Yeah, I know.'

'Once I came home from school crying like mad because Elaine Gibbs didn't want to be my friend any more—she said my feet were smelly—and do you know what Dad said?'

'What?'

'He said that Elaine would probably change her mind soon enough and he was right. By the next day she'd forgotten all about it and was friendly to me again. Dad said there's plenty of love to go around, enough for everyone, and he was right about that too, I reckon. You're the one-and-only Josh, and you guys will still have neat times together down at the cottage, Mrs D or no Mrs D. You'll always be Mr Patrick's special friend, no matter what.'

There was silence while Josh had a think about it. He drew a tiny cube with wings.

'Maybe.' He gave me a small smile. 'Thanks, Bec. By the way, did you know that there are more insects in one square mile of countryside than there are human beings on the whole planet?'

'Wow, that's pretty amazing. Now, little buddy, how about we get out the Boggle and have a major championship.'

So we did. Labelled diagrams of the central nervous system could wait. My brother was more important.

crazy love

It was dumb, right? You couldn't be in love with someone if you'd only met them once, could you? Although I had actually met Nick twice if you counted hanging out all evening with him and Jaz as once, and eating mangoes in the sun the next morning with him as twice. Anyhow, count it any way you want and call it what you like, infatuation or moonstruck or just plain loopy, some kind of strange magic had definitely taken place and my life now felt completely upside-down and sideways. That night my homework took double the usual length of time.

Infatuation is very time-consuming, I discovered. I looked in the mirror. There I was, Bec, with my red hair and brown eyes and oh no, the beginnings of a zit on my chin. It wasn't just your ordinary zit; the sort that pops a tiny white head up, the sort that you give a satisfying little squeeze and bung a bit of tea-tree oil on and zap, it's more or less gone. No, it was the worst sort of zit; the sort that takes days to come up and is very sore, the kind your finger wants to keep poking and prodding, the kind that makes your whole chin look bumpy and gross. And when you do actually squeeze it only half of it comes out and then it leaves a revolting icky blemish. I dabbed tea-tree oil on it with a cotton bud and prayed, because sometimes, if you are lucky and the goddesses are on your side, liberal applications of tea-tree oil and prayers will make a zit go away.

Next I concentrated on my hair in order to distract myself. I pinned it up every which way, trying for a glamorous style, and hunted in my drawers for the old blue velvet flower which I knew I had, somewhere. Finally I found it, then I had to hunt in Lewis's study for the superglue so I could glue the flower onto a hair comb. Lastly I had to pick the shreds of superglue off my fingers.

Now that I looked halfway decent, if you ignored my bumpy chin, I could begin my diagram, right? Wrong. I had more important things to do. I had to sit and replay every minute of my time at Jaz's house, but it didn't matter how many times I went over it, I couldn't get past two icky things. The first icky thing was that Nick was never going to like me the way I liked him already, because love at first sight wasn't going to happen when your first sight was of a goofy girl dressed in a saggy t-shirt and a pair of Cottontails, with mud and Clingwrap on her head; especially when the world was full of pretty girls, sophisticated girls, Uni girls, and funky girls.

That led me to the second icky thing, which was that Jaz said he wasn't interested in girls anyway. If Kuala Lumpur was full of gorgeous girls, groovy girls like Jaz, and he wasn't interested in any of them, then there was no way I had a chance. Me, plain ordinary Bec. I finished embellishing my elaborate design of tiny hearts and flowers surrounding a curly letter N and began my homework, but somehow it just didn't have the same gripping fascination as my daydreams. Mr Palmer wouldn't be very impressed if I handed in a page of curly-whirly stuff.

Love is like cow poo. Be careful or you will fall in it!

Having scribbled this on the back of an envelope I felt a bit better, and went to bed.

dreaming

I dreamed a garden. Roses, hundreds of roses, in every shade of wonderful. A dark green hedge with waxy white gardenias, as luminous as midnight stars. A row of pink tulips. Spiky cactus surrounding an Italian courtyard patterned with lavish coloured tiles. Carpets of dark shy violets. A waterlily pond.

Waking up was like falling from heaven and floating to earth.

I
   floated
      to
         earth
clutching
      a
         thought.

I would make a garden.

At school that day heaps of people commented on my hair. Gregory Mallory said The Dumbest Thing, which was 'everyone knows that redheads are sex maniacs'. Lisa kicked him for me, which I appreciated. Julia said The Best Thing, which was 'brilliant colour, Bec'. Julia's taste is so cool and her compliments are so infrequent that any praise from her is worth heaps.

I was hanging out to see Jaz, wondering if she'd say

anything about Nick. She isn't in the same Human Biology class as me so I didn't see her until third period. We always sit together in English Lit. Mr Buckley was away and we had a relief teacher. His name was Mr Cobb. Usually everyone kicks up when we have a relief teacher, but after Gregory Mallory called this dude Mr Knob and got a week's worth of detention we all quietened down. Mr Cobb was a tall skinny man with a beard and an unusual approach to his work. He said we could do anything we liked—catch up on our homework, or read, or do his poetry hand-outs—as long as we kept busy and didn't make any noise. Then he put his feet up on the desk and read *The Bulletin*. He was some strange dude, but it made for an easy class. Jaz and I grabbed a couple of poetry hand-outs and sat at the back talking quietly.

'It was fun that you came over. What did you do when you got home?' Jaz whispered.

'Strange things are happening in the suburbs,' I began, and proceeded to tell her the Patrick and Dawn saga.

'Are you pissed at her?' Jaz asked idly.

'Nah, not really. The more she focuses on him and the less notice she takes of me the better,' I answered. 'I never wanted a stupid housekeeper in the first place and she hasn't exactly turned out to be my kind of person.'

'Well, my mother woke up in a foul mood,' Jaz said, 'so Nick and I took off to the skate park in South Freo. It's a real scene there, you should see it. Nick was really going for it but then he snapped his deck. Seventy bucks for a new one, man, he goes through so many decks. We hung out for a while then Nick took off somewhere and I got the train home. Boring. But hey, he asked all about you though . . . somewhat strange for my I-don't-like-girls brother, don't you think?'

'What do you mean, "asked all about me"?' I hoped my voice was not coming out in an ultra-excited squeak.

'Well, you know, where you lived, and what you're into, and if you have a boyfriend.'

'You're kidding me, right?'

'No, why would I? But don't worry, I told him you weren't into guys.'

'Jaz!'

'What?'

'You didn't?'

'Sure. I mean that's what you told me, right?'

'Yeah, I know, but . . .'

'But?'

'But I think I might sort of like him.' Oh no! What on earth had I blurted it out for.

'Really?' asked Jaz.

'Yeah,' I mumbled.

'Oh.' There was a silence.

A long silence.

'You're not mad at me, are you, Jaz?' I asked.

'No, just surprised.'

More silence.

Jaz said she wasn't pissed off but she'd gone all quiet and I wasn't sure why.

'It won't make any difference though, to us, being friends, I mean,' I mumbled.

Sometimes words are like clumsy rocks. We both reached for the poetry hand-out at the same time, grinning at each other, because things were okay between us again.

WORKSHEET: WAYS OF SEEING

Poetry wakes us up. The world comes alive when words, images and ideas come together in ways that allow the reader room to respond with heart and mind. Read the following poem: *Thirteen Ways of Looking at a Blackbird*, by Wallace Stevens. Then compose a poem of your own, responding to an everyday object, using language in ways that will awaken the reader.

'Shall we do one together?' Jaz asked softly.

'Yeah, what shall we choose?'

'A pencil?'

'Nah.'

'An orange?'

'Nah.'

'Schoolbag?'

'Nah.'
'What then?'
'Umm, ah . . . a skateboard?'
'Cool.'

five ways of looking at a skateboard

among twenty city buildings
the only moving thing
was the skateboard

the skateboard whirled in the summer breeze
it was a small part of the pantomime

a boy and his cap
are one
a boy and his cap and his skateboard
are one

i do not know which to prefer
flying through the air
or just after

snap
deck busted
bugger

~~~

Jaz and I giggled. That Wallace Stevens dude better watch out.

~~~

At lunchtime my friends and I met at the usual spot. Jaz didn't have any lunch so we all shared but no one had anything exciting because it was Monday. I went and scored us a large choc milk and two buckets of chips from the canteen. It was great having money. Katherine was over the moon because Damian, the guy she met on the Net, said he might be coming over to Perth for a seminar in a few weeks. Julia showed us the gorgeous violet satin dress she got from Eros. Lisa lay down with her eyes shut. She looked pale and seedy.

'What's the matter?' Katherine asked.

'Piss off.' Lisa said it in a kind-of-joking way, but you could tell she wasn't going to answer Katherine properly. Katherine stared out at the sports field, trying to pretend that she wasn't hurt. There was an awkward silence.

'Guess what?' I asked. Might as well go for it and fill the gap with my big news. I left everyone guessing for a suitably tantalising length of time and then I spilled the beans about winning the money. They were most impressed. 'And get this. I'm going to make a garden,' I announced. 'Last night I had a dream about a magnificent garden. We've got this really daggy courtyard and I've decided to transform it into something glorious. When my parents come home it will be such a neat surprise for them.'

'Miss Bec-Goody-Two-Shoes,' said Lisa, in a really nasty tone.

'Don't be such a bitch,' I said. The words came out of my mouth before I had even had time to think. Jaz and Katherine and Julia just sat there in stunned silence. We'd never had a moment like this before.

'Oh shit, shit, shit,' said Lisa. 'I'm sorry, Bec. I didn't mean it.'

'What on earth is the matter with you, Lisa?' asked Julia.

'You name it and it's the matter,' Lisa replied, and then she told us everything. 'After work on Saturday I went to a party with Jeremy, who works at Really Good Burgers with me. He had some ecstasy tablets, Green Mitsubishi, and like an idiot I bought one off him. Actually he gave it to me and I was going to pay him later. It was a great night at first, but then I lost my wallet and I didn't get home until three. My mother went psycho. I haven't had any sleep and I still owe Jeremy the money, which I don't have.'

We all stared at her.

'How much did it cost?' asked Katherine, tentatively.

'Sixty bucks. I'll never do it again and that's for real. I mean, it was fun at first, no wonder they call it the happy drug, everything felt superb for a few hours. We were dancing like crazy, it was hell-fun, but now Jeremy thinks we're an item and I can't avoid seeing him because of work. My mother is completely hysterical, she's rabbiting on about me seeing a counsellor. She's the one who needs counselling, with her constant controlling. My life is a total mess.'

The siren went.

'I'm sorry, Bec. I didn't mean to take it out on you. Look, the garden sounds nice, it really does,' Lisa said. She looked contrite, as well as pale and seedy, so I decided to forgive her.

'It's cool,' I answered, and we all went our separate ways to class.

In French Mrs Tait set us a long, dense translation about two professors who had an incident involving an umbrella and a suitcase while travelling on the Metro in Paris. Whoopydee doo. I pretended to be busily working away and spent the next forty minutes on the metro track that was running round in my brain.

Talk about curly bits and knots and twists. I felt as if I was tumbling around in the wool basket, completely tangled up in skeins of red and orange and purple and yellow and blue and black and green. First my father had his breakdown. Then my parents went away. Out of the blue I won five hundred bucks. Reliable Mrs D and dear old Mr Patrick had vanished and in their place was the Dawn and Patrick Love Bug Show. Good old sensible Katherine had lost her vees. Lisa had got herself in a whole lot of trouble, and I had called her a bitch. I couldn't believe I'd done that, actually spat the dummy at her like that. Good old Bec, who's always nice to everyone. I didn't feel like good old Bec any more. I didn't know who the hell I felt like. And then there was Nick.

Nick the absolutely gorgeous.

Nick who maybe maybe maybe liked me, but who thought I didn't like him.

impossible flip

When I got home Mrs D was sitting at the table, slicing oranges deftly into a white china bowl.

'I'm getting these ready to make marmalade. They have to soak overnight. You wouldn't make a cup of tea, would you? My hands are all sticky. There's some Tim Tams in the cupboard.

'So, life's full of surprises, isn't it?' said Mrs D companionably when I sat down. 'Since my husband died six years ago there's just been me and work and my dogs. And now this. It feels rather nice to have an admirer.'

'Mmmm,' I answered, dipping a Tim Tam in my tea. You have to be very careful about timing when dipping a Tim Tam. If you leave it too long all the coating melts away, but if you catch it at just the right moment you get a delicious chocolate mouth-explosion of delight. I took a last satisfying crunchy bite and concentrated on licking my sticky fingers.

'You don't mind, do you, Bec? I know your parents would be okay with this, I mean there isn't any funny business going on.'

'No, um, of course not,' I replied.

For the first time since she arrived with her daggy old suitcases I felt friendly towards her. These were strange times, however. The housekeeper was asking me if she was allowed to have a boyfriend. Wasn't it supposed to be the other way around?

'Mr Patrick's lovely, go for it. Umm, how did your husband die?' I asked, to change the subject.

'It was very sudden. He was at a calligraphy workshop and he got a pain in his chest. The tutor sent him to the hospital, just in case, and the doctors found a tiny split in his aorta. They kept him in overnight and did a few tests, told us it was nothing to worry about. They were going to send him home but when he got out of bed to get dressed his aorta ripped, and he died.'

'Oh no. How awful. Were you there?'

'I was down the hall, talking to the nurse. Just a minute before I had been with him and we were laughing together. "A lot of fuss about nothing, I'm perfectly fine and the sooner I get home the better, sweetie," he said. The next minute he was gone.'

'Oh,' I said.

'I know it sounds corny, Bec, but it made me appreciate how precious life is. We think we have for ever but sometimes we don't.'

'Mmm,' I answered. I felt closer to Mrs D now that she had shared important stuff with me, but I felt embarrassed too. It was almost too up close and personal. I didn't want to think about death. The only death I had experienced was when my grandmother died. I was six. I remembered the fragrance of gardenias at her funeral, and everyone being serious and sad. Sometimes when grown-ups try to talk about deep and meaningful stuff I feel edgy, like they're trying to tell me things that I need to sort out for myself.

'Where are Josh and Bing?' I asked, to change the subject again.

'Josh is down at the cottage, and Bing is over at Megan's house. So, how was your day, Bec?' Mrs D asked, pouring herself some more tea.

'Not bad, I guess.'

'I wondered, because you don't seem quite yourself. Is everything okay?'

Mrs D must be psychic or something. I thought I'd been acting perfectly normal, despite the turmoil in my brain. I couldn't decide whether to fob her off or talk to her. Oh, what the hell.

'Well, things *are* a bit crazy at the moment. One of my friends got herself into a bundle of trouble, and it's just been a very strange sort of a day.'

'She's not preggie, is she?'

'Oh no, nothing like that.'

Mrs D began clearing the table. 'By the way, your friend Jaz rang you just before you got home. I said you'd call her back.'

~~~

I grabbed the portable phone. Sped up the stairs. Kicked my shoes off. Peeled my school skirt and blouse off with one hand. Sprawled out on my bed, amongst my big comfy pillows, in my pale blue underwear. Bliss.

'Hey, Jaz.'

'Hi, Bec, how are you? I mean, today was kind of bizarre, right, with Lisa?'

'For sure.'

'Are you annoyed with her?'

'Nah, not too much. She's in deep trouble though.'

'That's for sure, I wouldn't like to be her right now, no way. Anyhow, here's the thing, do you want to come to a skate demo on Saturday. It's at God Park.'

'What?'

'God Park. Nick and all his friends are going. It's a skate park up the coast, at Whitfords. We could get a ride with Nick and his friend Steve, that's if you want to come. I've never been to one, but they're meant to be hell-fun.'

'Yeah, for sure. I'll have to check it out with Mrs D first but she'll probably be cool. I might not tell her how we're getting there though, I'll say we're going on the bus. Maybe you could come back to my house afterwards and stay the night?'

'I'll run it past my old lady and tell you tomorrow, okay?'

'Cool.'

MONDAY AFTER PHONE CALL: Ask Mrs D about Saturday. Tell her we're catching the bus. Yes, I can go. Brilliant. No, Jaz is not allowed to stay over. Bummer.

TUESDAY AFTER SCHOOL: Try on all my clothes. Decide to wear my blue jeans and white t-shirt, and wear my hair up with the blue velvet flower comb. Happiness.

WEDNESDAY AFTER SCHOOL: My parents ring from Chicago. I suddenly feel guilty about Saturday but say nothing. Eat five Tim Tams. Feel vaguely ill.

THURSDAY AFTER SCHOOL: Try on all my clothes again and decide everything is revolting. Try on all Vera's clothes. Nothing fits me except her best cream silk shirt, which looks really sexy but which would look crap at a skate demo. Panic. Ignore homework. Watch junk TV all night. Feel better. Squeeze zit. Feel worse.

FRIDAY AFTER SCHOOL: Try on all my clothes. Decide to wear my blue jeans and white t-shirt, and wear my hair up with blue velvet flower comb.

On Friday night I couldn't sleep. I lay awake thinking about the garden. Lisa saying it was a crappy idea had bent my head right out of shape. Okay, maybe she was in a shitty and didn't totally mean it, but her comment had dug a little hole in my heart none the less. Perhaps the garden *was* a dumb idea. Maybe I *was* just a goodie-goodie girl. Bec who helped her mother with the cooking. Bec who did her homework on time. Bec who never took any risks. Bec, the sensible one. Bec the ordinary. Bec the dull.

sky blue saturday

We go. We go up the turquoise coast in Steve's purple Beetle with hell-cool music playing: Moby and Air and The Red Hot Chilli Peppers. When Nick says 'hey Bec' and smiles that just-for-me smile, I feel as radiant as the Goddess of the Planet of Blue Velvet Flowers. Steve cranks up the tunes. He's a friendly guy with loopy blond hair and tattoo of a fish on his wrist. Jaz and I sit in the back seat. Nick's slender arm stretches along the back of the front seat. His skin is as smooth as chocolate. I want to reach out and touch it, lick it even.

When we get to God Park there are dozens of guys skating and zooming and zipping and flipping everywhere and crashing and carrying on while the organisers try to get everyone off the ramps so the competition can begin. It's total mayhem.Nick and Steve pay their two bucks entry fee and join the crowd of whizzing skaters practising their tricks and generally showing off big-time.

Finally the ramp is cleared and the show begins. Each skater gets two runs and forty-five seconds to perform their best manoeuvres. The heats go by the ages of the skaters. The ten year olds go first. Jaz and Steve and Nick and I hang out under a tree, watching. I attempt to learn the difference between an ollie, a nollie, a back-side kick flip, a back-side heel flip, a back-side ollie, a front-side ollie and an impossible flip. It's mad fun.

We stay for hours. It's hot. We drink Coke and I wish I was wearing a flexicap and cargo pants and a Boom t-shirt like everyone else. I ask why not many girls skate. Steve says it's because they don't like getting hurt. Jaz says 'no way' but she can't think of a better reason. Nick tells us about a top girl skater called Elissa Steamer who can nollie backside down eight stairs and over a chain, which is incredibly impressive. I tell them that my friend, Eloise, who lives in New York, is a skater. Then we discuss why not many girls are DJs. No one can think of a good reason. Jaz says she wants to be one. Then Steve has his turn. He's really going for it but he snaps his deck. Jaz says maybe girls don't skate because they're too sensible to waste seventy bucks a week on a flimsy piece of board. Steve tells us about some American boards that are made out of special stuff and are way stronger but cost a hundred and sixty bucks. Nick has his turn and he is brilliant but he doesn't win because another guy is even better. My head is spinning from all the Coke and all the whizzing and then we have to head back because Steve's brother needs his car.

HOW TO KICKFLIP

The kickflip is a common and fundamentally beautiful skateboarding manoeuvre. If successful, the board flips a full three hundred and sixty degrees and is caught back under your feet while you and the board are still in the air. The front foot, which can be either the left or right foot depending on whether your stance is natural or goofy, is placed with the toe just touching the bottom bolt of the front four. Bottom left for goofy, bottom right for natural. This trick, like most, can be done at a variety of speeds.

0km/hour is called stationary and is the best way to learn the trick. Starting on grass can ease the pain but involves more effort to get the board to pop up. 30km/hour is only for those with extreme skill and little fear for their own safety. As a rule of thumb the faster you do it the better it feels and the riskier it is.

The first part of the trick is to ollie. This is the most fundamental move of skating, allowing the rider to defy gravity. All other flips and tricks are skilled variations on the theme. When this trick was first invented, other skateboarders accused the rider of having Velcro pads attached to the board and his shoes, but once understood this trick revolutionised the sport. The only way to learn it is by hours of practice, kicking the tail down with the back foot and then at precisely the right time jumping and pushing the front of the board down until the board is horizontal. Success will be evident by the fact that you and your board are in the air together, feeling fine. Some professional skaters have mastered this to an amazing extent, like Kien Leui, who can ollie over a road block—useful if you need to make a quick getaway through a police roadblock.

Now you can ollie, back to the kickflip. As you and the board make your way up into the air, it's time to implement the second phase of the manoeuvre. Instead of merely sliding your foot up the board to bring the board level, as for an ollie, you whip the front foot up and cunningly flick just enough to make the board flip over. The board is then caught with the back foot, causing it to stop rotating. The front foot comes back from where you flung it to execute the flip and then you land and roll away, feeling a sense of superb achievement. Once mastered on flat ground the kickflip can, with practice, be put to a variety of uses, from kickflipping down sets of stairs, to doing eight-foot airs on a vertical ramp.

sunday morning

I woke up. Tea Party was playing too loudly somewhere nearby. My head hurt. Jaz was asleep beside me. I recognised her tousled head sticking out of a green sleeping bag. Jimmy Hendrix and The Doors were watching us from the walls. I sat up, wearing only my white t-shirt and my undies. I smelled pretty rank. Oh no, it was coming back to me now.

Steve had to get the car back so we all ended up at his place, a grotty brick and tile house in the suburbs. I didn't even know what suburb I was in but it certainly wasn't Dalkieth.

Steve's mother said 'Hi, kids, call me Janice.' She finished her ironing, then went out. The fridge was full of beer in tall brown bottles and we all got stuck in to it. It tasted foul but I drank it anyway. After the first glass it didn't matter what it tasted like, you just felt fine.

I rang Mrs D and told her I was staying over at Jaz's house. It was almost too easy. She just said, 'Okay, dear, see you tomorrow.' We drank more beer. Steve made a great pile of baked bean jaffles with white bread in an old sandwich maker. What happened next? . . . oh, that's right. Nick took off with Steve's brother to try and score some mull. 'See ya soon', Nick said, but they never came back . . . not that I remember. Jaz and Steve and I hung out for awhile, having fun and talking bullshit.

Here comes the dodgy bit.

It was really late. Jaz fell asleep. I sat on the back step with Steve, looking up at the hugeness of the sky. The night was dancing with stars whose names we didn't remember so we named them ourselves: Madonna's Underpants, The Teapot, Bright-Star-All-Alone. Steve scruffled around in his pocket and produced the remains of a very squashed joint. I didn't want to say I'd never smoked before so I took big puffs and tried not to cough. Things got pretty spinny after that. We laughed a lot and Steve told me this bizarre story about how he got his fish tattoo, and then he put his arm around me. It took me by surprise, but if felt good. Sort of awkward and easy all at the same time. I liked the way he smelled, like sweat and sandalwood.

Then we were kissing. I wanted to, sort of. I wanted to know what kissing someone was like, and I didn't know how to get out of it without embarrassing both of us. Also I was mad at Nick for taking off into the night in search of drugs and not coming back. The kissing thing wasn't very successful though. It started out sort of gentle and pleasant but then Steve started rubbing his body against me. His hand was fumbling around looking for my bra strap. Things were going way too fast and the beer and the dope was making me a bit spewy, so I said I needed to lie down. Steve went inside and I crashed. End of story.

How I wished that was the end of the story. Confusion city. How did I get myself into this mess?

I wanted Jaz to wake up and talk to me.

'Go away, no, no, not *The River*, anything but that,' she howled, and hid under the bedclothes.

After a while she surrendered to my cunning wiles and popped her head out of the sleeping bag. Her hair was all mussed up and tufty like a scarecrow girl. 'Life is a game and I don't know how to play it,' I said. My mouth felt all furry.

'One day I will teach you how to play Mah-jong,' Jaz said wisely, and went back to sleep. Maybe I was still a bit stoned because even though it didn't quite make sense it made perfect sense. 'Good', I answered, directing my words to Jimi

Hendrix and Jim Morrison because Jaz had deserted me again.

I imagine my fingers clattering small ivory tiles. I'm a Mah-jong Queen, in a silk kimono and embroidered slippers. I am fragrant with sandalwood. For one delicious moment I am a very elegant Hong Kong girl of nineteen who lives with Nick. He adores me.

Wake up, girl. It can never happen. Nick will find out I pashed up Steve. He'll hate me. It's too late. I have stuffed everything up.

I lay down for a while, wishing I was dead. Well, maybe not dead but on a tropical island far from this crappy shed. Okay, Bec, admit it, it isn't the shed that's crappy. It's you. Why did you pash up the wrong guy, a guy you hardly knew? Just because you were shit-faced, that's no excuse.

'Morning, girls.' A cheery voice interrupted my misery. It was Steve's mum, in an orange tracksuit, proudly bearing a tray with two steaming mugs on it. 'Made you some Nescafé, hope you both take milk and sugar . . . figured you might need a bit of rocket fuel. Steve and Andrew have gone to soccer. They said to say bye, and Nick caught a ride with them . . . said he'd see you at home, Jaz. I have to go in to the city, I can drop you at the train station or somewhere if you like.'

Who the heck is Andrew, I wondered, then I remembered. Oh yeah, Steve's brother, Mr Purple Volkswagen himself. Jaz and I stumbled out of bed and into our clothes. The coffee was too sweet and too milky but it sure hit the spot.

'What are we doing here?' I asked.

Jaz grinned. 'Beats staying home with the telly, my friend,' she replied, fumbling for her Docs.

Janice tooted loudly from the driveway. We hopped into her rusty red Corolla and sped down the freeway, the river dancing like blue diamonds, all the way to the city. Janice popped a tape in, and Tea Party blatted out once more. 'Love this one, girls, don't you?'

'Mmmm,' said Jaz. Safe in the back seat, I stared out the window, trying not to burst out laughing.

~~~~

Jaz and I didn't get a chance to talk at the train station. Her train left almost straight away. I was glad. I needed time to think.

'See ya, call ya later,' Jaz yelled, sprinting towards the closing doors.

It took me ages to get home. I got off my train at the deserted station and waited forty minutes for the bus to the hills. Stupid Sundays. I walked slowly back from the bus stop, looking at tree bark and cobwebs and tiny purple bush orchids. Natural things usually make me feel alive and good, but not this time. I wished that last night hadn't happened but wishing wouldn't undo things, and worse was yet to come.

'Hello, Bec. Did you have a good time at Jaz's house?' Mrs D's voice met me before I was even in the door properly.

I could tell by her frosty tone that I was in deep shit.

'Yep.'

'Oh, that's odd, Bec, because Mrs Lim rang me last night, it was nearly midnight, she was very distressed, Jaz and Nick hadn't come home and she didn't know where they were.'

I could have tried to lie my way out of it and said we got home right after that, but I couldn't be bothered.

'I'm very disappointed in you, Bec. I thought I could trust you but obviously I can't. I'll talk to you later.'

'Fine.' I headed up to have a shower. No use saying anything. She wouldn't understand.

the big awful

By the time I came downstairs in search of food, Mrs D and Josh had gone down to the cottage to say goodbye to Mr Patrick, who was flying to Broome or somewhere to visit his son. Bing hung around looking lonesome and bored.

'Play with me, Bec,' she begged, 'we could dress Begonia and Eggleton up in the dolls' clothes, make a wedding or a party, please?'

'Nah, Bingo, you'll have to watch the box or something, I've got homework,' I lied.

I made a large sandwich smeared with butter, peanut butter and great dobs of apricot jam and went back up to my room to hide from my lies. I hopped into bed but my head was a rat's nest of regret and misery, so I got up and took out my art stuff.

I cut out a stone angel, an old chair, seven yellow roses, and a sleeping cat. I stuck them on to a picture of a garden, a grove of dark leafy trees with white Chinese paper lanterns hanging from the branches. I make a safe place, and I rest there a while, drifting like a moth with blue wings amongst the canopy of leaves.

'Help, Bec, come quickly. Help!'

It took me a few seconds to remember that I was not a languid moth. With a last flutter of my blue wings I returned to Planet Perth. Outside my bedroom window I saw Josh, running up the path, yelling like crazy.

'Bec, Bec, you have to come.' He was puffing and breathless, face pale as dust.

'Josh, sit down. What is it? What's happened?' I tried to sound steady but I was already panicking. My stomach was a hollow box of fear.

'It's Mrs D! She's hurt herself. Mr Patrick went to the airport in a taxi and me and Mrs D were walking home and she fell down a great big hole. Her leg is really bad. It looks all wonky. We gotta go there.'

'Let's go on the bikes,' said Bing, who had appeared out of nowhere.

Good old Bing, my smart little sister. I wanted to hug her, but there was no time.

~~~

We pedalled faster than we had ever pedalled before. Josh led the way. We zoomed around a corner and there was Mrs D, lying awkwardly in a bed of leaves by the side of the road. A pale blue Volvo came zooming around the corner.

'Wave it down,' Bing bellowed, so we all waved frantically.

'What's up, kids?' asked the Volvo woman, looking worried.

'It's our housekeeper, she's hurt, she's over here,' said Josh, and we hurried to where Mrs D lay.

It's odd the things you remember in a crisis. I can still see the incongruous sight of Mrs D's squashy rainbow raffia handbag hanging neatly on a low branch beside her.

'Are you all right, Mrs D?' Bing asked.

'Not quite all right. Don't worry, pet, I'm going to be fine, but I think I've broken my leg.' Mrs D tried to grin but her face was grey and her teeth were gritted. 'That bloody hole. I pulled myself out but only just.'

We all stared down at the deep concrete hole. It looked like a big old drainage pipe or something.

'Oh, how dangerous. My name is Kaye, by the way. I'll ring for an ambulance,' said the Volvo lady, as she pulled her mobile phone out of her purse. I've always thought mobile phones were a wank, but I was very glad to see one right then.

The ambulance zoomed up, pulsing with noise and light, just like in the movies. Josh was most impressed. Two paramedics jumped out: an older guy with a tangle of curly hair, a younger one with a silver earring and no hair at all. They took charge of everything. Mrs D was strapped to a stretcher and given an injection for the pain.

'Looks like a double fracture, and a pretty nasty one to boot,' said Tangles.

'Okay, darling, let's get you in and get you x-rayed,' said Baldie, and away they went, siren blaring once more.

'Where do you live, kids? I'll drive you home,' said Kaye, but she looked a bit frantic, as if she was meant to be somewhere else.

'No, it's fine, we have our bikes,' I said, sounding more sensible and calm than I actually felt.

'Your parents are at home, aren't they?'

'Yes, for sure, we'll be fine, we don't live far away,' I said. 'Thank you for helping us, see ya.'

I didn't dare look at Bing and Josh until the Volvo was safely out of sight. They were both staring at me solemnly.

'Bec, what a whopper,' said Bing.

'Sometimes you have to fudge it,' I replied. 'Come on, let's get home and decide what we're going to do.'

big scary decisions

The first thing I did when we got home was to make a pot of tea and get out the Tim Tams. Maybe chocolate would help me think. I made Josh and Bing's tea milky and weak, children's tea, Vera calls it, but I made mine good and strong. Vera's favourite blue-and-white speckled teapot sat cosily on the table. There is something very reassuring about a teapot. Bing stirred three spoons of sugar into her tea. I didn't tell her not to, you can't die of a sugar overdose as far as I know.

'What are we going to do, Bec?' Josh's eyes were all owly behind his glasses. I realised I'd hardly seen him lately. Bing was looking at me as well. Her poodle hair had nearly grown out, but her feisty expression was still as total as ever.

'Well, we should ring Aunty Helen, I suppose,' I sighed. The thought of life with Aunty Helen was not a happy thought. Aunty Helen is Lewis's sister. She lives in Sydney, but she'd be on the plane in a minute if we picked up the phone and called her. Don't get me wrong, Aunty Helen is sort of okay but she's nothing like my father. The word serene can't be used to describe Aunty Helen, she isn't the easiest person to be around. Vera says that when the electrician in the sky did the wiring he wired Aunty Helen a bit too tightly. She smokes about a packet of cigarettes a day and talks pretty much non-stop, mainly about boring stuff like her clients, her hairdresser and her bank balance. After an hour or so in my aunt's company you feel like you need a week in Bali to recover. Also, she means well, but she brings us the completely wrong sort of presents, like a Britney Spears CD for me, or a soccer ball for Josh, who is the least sporty boy in Perth. She never listens to a word my brother says, and she tries to take Bing shopping for department store clothes, 'girls-wear' she calls it, which Bing does not appreciate in the least.

'Get real,' said Bing.

Josh was looking flabbergasted. That made three of us who didn't think much of the Aunty Helen idea.

'What else could we do?' asked Josh.

'We could ring Neil and Linda, I suppose.' Neil and Linda are Vera and Lewis's best friends. They're cool. They don't have any kids. They have tropical fish instead, because fish don't wear nappies and they can't talk back. They live in Mandurah, where they run a restaurant, a funky one with Mediterranean food and jazzy music.

'We'd probably have to go and stay with them, wouldn't we, because of Eggplant?' asked Bing.

I laughed. 'The restaurant is called Aubergine, not Eggplant, Bingo, and yeah, we probably would, but it'd be a total hassle. We'd have to travel for hours each day to get to school, even if Linda could drive us, which I doubt.'

We sat quietly, deep in the wilderness of our own thoughts.

'Mrs D is probably going to be in hospital for ages with a fracture that bad,' said Josh.

'We need a calendar,' I said, 'and a piece of paper. How many days is it until Vera and Lewis come home?'

We counted. Ten days.

'There's just this week,' I said, 'and then next weekend, and then they get home on the following Tuesday.'

<u>CHOICES</u>, I wrote, in my neatest printing.
1. Ring Aunty Helen.
2. Ring Neil and Linda.
3. Tell Vera and Lewis.

I crossed out Number One and Number two. We looked at Number Three from every possible angle. We could wait until Vera and Lewis phoned, which would probably be soon. Or we could ring them. Bing fetched the list of contact numbers from the fridge door. It seemed like for ever since Vera had stuck them there with her angel magnets. Our parents were in Chicago at the Blackstone Hotel, just about to leave for their final week in Taos, New Mexico, the place they always dreamed of visiting. We could call them tonight at the Hacienda del Sol. I remembered Vera raving on about it when she got the brochure, how it had adobe walls, a view of Taos Mountain and a hot tub.

Bing and Josh and I looked at each other glumly. 'If we tell them what's happened it will utterly wreck their dream holiday,' I said. 'Vera will be on the plane in an instant.'

'They might find us another housekeeper, through an agency or something,' Josh added doubtfully.

'I know Vera, she'll ring Aunty Helen,' Bing contributed, even more doubtfully. She made a face. 'I couldn't stand ten days with that woman. She'd yap yap yap all the time, and try and make me wear a pink skirt and top from Aherns. I refuse,' she declared dramatically.

Bing reached over for the piece of paper. We were all thinking the same thing but she was the one to write it down.

CHOICES
1. Ring Aunty Helen.
2. Ring Neil and Linda.
3. Tell Vera and Lewis.
4. Not tell any one.

We sat quietly again. Thinking. I couldn't tell what Bing and Josh were thinking but I was thinking, why not?

Josh got the envelope and made another list. He loves lists.

THINGS TO DO
Ring the hospital. See how Mrs D is. Visit her. Take her nice flowers.
Go to school.
Look after the animals.
Wash our clothes.
Buy food.

He looked up, worried. 'What about money?'

'I have money,' I told him. 'I have four hundred and fifty-nine dollars and seventy-eight cents in cash. It's hidden in the pocket of my purple dressing gown at the back of my wardrobe.'

'Yeah, in your dreams, Bec,' said Bing.

So I told them the story of the money. They were most impressed. By the time we'd made another list of what food we had and what we needed to buy, and a list of who was going to do the chores, we were hungry. I made a pile of ham-and-cheese sandwiches and we ate them while we watched *Third Rock From the Sun*.

'This is so good,' said Bing. 'Just us, right?'

'Yeah,' said Josh. The way he said it I wondered if he was totally okay with our plan. To tell the truth, I wasn't altogether sure about it myself but I had to act strong and certain so that Josh and Bing would feel safe. I'd think about it properly later, when they were in bed.

~~~

Bing was in full-tilt zap pow mode. She was feeling fine and frisky.

'I refuse to have a shower. I'm not dirty enough yet, Bec,' she declared.

I was too tired to argue with her. She danced around her bedroom in her South Park pyjamas, and then tucked in under her doona with *Harry Potter*. Eggleton lay curled at her feet, sleek and black.

'I can read as long as I want to tonight, even until midnight,' Bing announced, and promptly fell asleep.

I stuck my head round Josh's door. He was propped up with pillows, as serious as a small otter, absorbed in an *Omni* magazine.

'I'm going to ring the hospital,' I told him. 'I'll be back in a minute.'

I found the number in the fat white phone book and was just about to begin dialling when the phone rang, startling me. It rang louder than usual, or perhaps it just seemed that way. It was Jaz.

'Guess what?' she asked, and didn't wait for a reply. 'That guy, the cool one, the one in Dada—the handsome one with the glasses—got on the train, and he sat by me and we talked all the way home. His name is Sam, he's an Art student and he's *really* nice. We did the phone number thing, swapped them . . .'

'Wow.'

'The thing is,' Jaz continued excitedly, 'should I ring him or wait for him to ring me—I mean what if he doesn't? I should wait at least until Wednesday, maybe even Friday . . . what do you think?'

'Yeah,' I responded. I knew it wasn't an appropriate reply but my mind had turned to mush. The events of the day had caught up with me. So this was what shock was like: grey and empty, like there is no one home.

'Bec, what's up? You sound kind of funny.'

I tell Jaz what has happened, just the bare bones of it. 'I've got some stuff to do, see you at school, okay?'

'Sure, no worries. Take it easy, bye.'

The ward clerk at the hospital was briskly helpful. 'The patient is comfortable and her progress is very satisfactory. She's asleep right now, but if you ring back in the morning you can talk to her yourself,' she chirped.

Josh was lying in the dark on his back, his magazine abandoned amongst the pile of pillows on the floor. I plonked myself in the beige beanbag and gave him the hospital report.

'She's going to be fine, there's nothing to worry about, Josh Bosh.'

'Okay,' came his sleepy reply.

Silence. A deep dark blue soft silence.

'Bec?' my brother murmurs.

'What?'

I hold my breath. He's going to say that we should tell Vera and Lewis. I'm dreading it, because I half agree with him. My sensible half, that is. The other half of me doesn't wish to be sensible. The other Bec, the new half, wants to dance in satin underwear in the moonlight and never be sensible ever again. She wants to learn to do a kickflip on a skateboard, to turn up at school with a bad attitude and a bizarre excuse instead of a completed assignment. She wants to ignore salad, and eat sticky cake for lunch instead. She wants to get a tiny tattoo of a tulip on her shoulder. She wants to cuddle up with someone who understands her secret heart, to talk until morning about a million different things.

Josh's voice slid gently through the night, returning me to Planet Normal. 'Did you know that a duck's quack doesn't echo? No one knows why. Isn't that strange?'

'Very strange, darling boy. It's time for sleep now, so goodnight.' I reached out and clumsily patted the nearest bit of him that I could find, which turned out to be his knee.

I went downstairs and locked all the doors. I wasn't frightened. This house had always been safe. What else should I do, now that I was in charge? Even though I wanted to be a different girl, a wild and dancing kind of a girl, I still had a very practical streak, it seemed. I looked in the bread-bin. Only a few slices left. Never mind, we could have cereal for breakfast and buy our lunches with money from my dressing-gown-pocket stash.

In the comfort of my bedroom I lit the two vanilla scented candles Bing gave me for Christmas. I'd been saving them for some time special. Now felt special. I sat at my desk and looked out the window, into the cool satiny darkness.

The night had its own friendly sounds: faint cricket chirp and bird call, and the hum of the cars on the distant highway that snaked down towards the city. It was gentle, outside in the night. It was gentle inside me, too. Somehow it was as though there were two Becs, two ways of looking at things, two voices mingling like a river inside my head. One of them said 'ring your parents'. The other one said 'no way'. It's not like the two voices were fighting, though. It was as if the calmness of the night was big enough to hold them both. I cleaned my teeth and put on my satin nightgown, the slinky petticoat one with tiny straps, my movie-star nighty. I stretched out in bed. My eyes felt heavy, sleepy, and my body did, too. Everything was peaceful and dreamy. 'In the morning we'll get up and eat breakfast and it will taste good', I said to myself. 'We'll get dressed and cycle to school just like we always do. Right now everything is okay. Everything is exactly how it is supposed to be. I will decide what to do tomorrow,' I tell myself, like Scarlett did in *Gone with the Wind*. Scarlett is a good name . . . it's a colour and a name . . . what are other colour names? Well, there's Rose and there's Amber . . . there's Silver, but only if you're a horse. Rainbow would be a good name for a hippie girl . . . I wriggled my toes, and drifted towards the sweetness of sleep.

the best laid plans

Far out. I slept in. It is late late late late. 'Get up, Bing.' 'Get up, Josh.' 'Bloody well get up, Bing.' We gobbled our muesli, racing the clock. Josh couldn't find his homework book. We scrabbled around, searching furiously, getting in each other's way, but no luck. 'Josh, get your shoes on, we have to go, as in *right now*, dude.' Holy Moly, here's the homework book, underneath Bing's sneakers. Grab our schoolbags, grab some money. Oh no, it's twenty past eight. We have to dash run fly whizz go go go go go. No time to ring the hospital. I'll do it after school. Lock the door. 'Come on, you guys, we're so late.'

At the corner, we ground our bikes to a halt, and I handed Bing and Josh some lunch money.

'Four bucks each. Get something healthy. Chicken salad rolls, and an orange juice, or something.'

'Yeah right,' said Bing.

I could see her mentally adding up whether she had enough for a bottle of Coca Cola, and two Chiko rolls.

'Come straight home after school,' I added.

'Can Megan come over?' Bing asked.

'Not today, Bingo, maybe tomorrow.' If Megan found out what's happened she'd tell her mother for sure, and then we'd be stuffed. I had no idea whether tomorrow would be any safer, but stalling for time seemed like a good plan.

~~~~

I might as well have skipped Human Biology that morning. Mr Palmer's fascinating explanation of the genetic code and protein synthesis could have floated right out the window and landed in the petunia bed far as I was concerned. I stuffed up my French dictation completely as well. Mrs Tait was not impressed.

'C'est pathétique, Bec,' she said crossly.

'Oui, Madame,' I answered, trying to look pale and ill, as though I had period pains or something.

At lunchtime I hurried to the canteen to get something to

eat. I looked at the chicken salad rolls. Very nice. Very healthy. Very boring.

'Two cinnamon buns with butter, a large packet of corn chips and a Coffee Chill, please. But don't tell my sister,' I added under my breath.

'What's that, dear?' asked Mrs Johnson, the canteen lady, as she handed me my food and took my money. Mrs Johnson is a big wobbly woman with a dodgy perm but she's rather cheery and likeable.

'Nothing. Thanks, Mrs Johnson,' I answered, and dashed off to meet my friends.

When Julia and Lisa and Katherine and Jaz arrived we crunched into the corn chips, and I blurted out the saga of the accident and Mrs D being in hospital.

'So, wise girls, what do you reckon I should do? I mean, I sort of want to tell someone and I sort of don't.'

'I think you should phone your parents, Bec,' said Katherine. 'I mean, they'll find out when they get home, won't they, and then you'll be in a shit-load of trouble.'

'No way,' said Julia. 'Definitely *do not* tell anyone, just do your own thing. Ten days without any adults will be, like, totally amazing. And what can they do once they get back? I mean, it'll be too late by then, anyhow, right? They might even be really impressed by how you showed your independence.'

Jaz and Lisa said nothing. Well, that isn't exactly true. Jaz sat cross-legged, grinning like some kind of flame-haired gnome, and told everyone about meeting Sam on the train.

'Shall I ring him or wait till he rings me?' she asked plaintively. Jaz's hair blazed like an electric beacon. She looked happy and bemused and terrified all at the same time. Last week Jaz and I were normal human beings, now we were both upside-down and sideways. Maybe someone had put love juice in the water.

'I have it!' said Lisa. 'This is the way it has to be. Bec doesn't tell anyone, right? Forget Helen, the aunt from hell, and why drag your parents home for no reason? Getting along by yourselves will be sweet, you can handle it, ten days is nothing. And as for Sam, Jaz can ring him and ask him to the party.'

'Party?' the four of us ask in unison.

'Yeah, the *party*. Saturday night. Let's have a party. At Bec's. There'll be the five of us, and Jaz can invite Sam, right? I mean, if he doesn't ring her, it gives her the perfect excuse to ring him. Bec can invite Jaz's brother, so we can all feast our eyes on this incredible spunk, and maybe he can bring one or two of his skateboarding mates, so Julia and I can fall in love or lust with someone, seeing everyone else is. I can get a ride with Jeremy from the burger bar. He's not that bad, sometimes he's quite fun and it'll help to even up the numbers. We can all make some party food, and bring some tunes. It'll be magic.'

Like a row of gaudy clowns with open mouths and swivelling heads, Jaz and Lisa and Katherine and Julia turned to look at me. I was topsy-turvey with terror and excitement.

'Sure,' I said. 'Let's do it, why not?'

'Oh my God,' shrieked Katherine, in her usual over-the-top style. 'I wish Damian could come but now he isn't sure if he can afford the ticket to Perth because he just had to pay three hundred dollars to the vet when his dog got run over and broke its leg,' she continued.

'Too bad, maybe you can fall in lerve with a skateboarder, or there's always the dreaded Jeremy,' said Lisa.

'Spew city,' says Katherine, looking vaguely hurt but not hurt enough to freak out about it.

So then we get into a huge excitable discussion about music. Lisa likes very bizarre bands like The Super Furry Animals from Wales. 'I'll bring a couple of their albums,' she offered.

Jaz is into house music and acid jazz, and says she'll bring her Madison Avenue CD. Katherine, whose musical taste is rather bland, looked blank. She's never heard of any of our more obscure musical discoveries. 'Well, I think we should have lots of dance music. My parents have got The Greatest Dance Hits of the Seventies, I could bring that along,' she offered.

'You're kidding. No way. That is just so absolutely totally *not* a good idea,' argued Lisa. Katherine opened her mouth to disagree but I got in first.

'Now now, girls, no fighting. Bring along whatever you like and we can take turns at being DJ.' This is the cool thing.

When the party is at your house, you get to be the Power Queen and have the final say.

Julia acted really bored about the music. As usual she was more interested in clothes. We spent a long time debating whether she should wear her blue lace hippie dress, or maybe her new violet skirt with the pink stretchy top.

'What about food?' I asked. 'We have to have good munchies.' Right then the siren interrupted, with its usual nasty piercing screech.

'To be continued,' Lisa said.

'For sure,' we agreed, and ambled off into the warm sleepy afternoon.

I longed to stretch out on my bed, put on my Sofa King album and snooze off for a couple of hours but instead Mr Buckley, our regular English Lit teacher, has returned, and he wants us to discuss *A Streetcar Named Desire* with a passion way beyond our capabilities.

'You have read it, people, haven't you?' he entreated. 'You know you were supposed to have read it by today.' He looked at us balefully and blew his nose in an unnecessarily trumpety manner. I wish he had stayed home and had a long snooze as well. Mr Cobb was far more restful to the soul.

I am in need of a deep think.

My mind floats in and out of the stuffy classroom, like a green butterfly drifting in a field of sunflowers . . . 'representation of women' says Mr Buckley . . . *as soon as I get home I must ring the hospital,* I remind myself . . . 'identity and alienation' . . . *what on earth are we going to have for tea tonight? on the way home I'll stop at the supermarket and get some stuff I hope I brought enough money* . . . 'point of view shift' . . . *oh help have I done the right thing perhaps I should ring Vera and Lewis* . . . 'narrative device' . . . *but a party will be just so fun* . . . 'where is meaning located?' . . . *what if Nick doesn't come I really want him to but what about Steve oh what a mess* . . . 'cultural assumptions' . . . *blooming Julia and her obsession with clothes I have no idea what I am going to wear maybe I can borrow something from Julia* . . . 'let's look at the cultural meaning of tongue studs. Bec, can you give us your opinion please?' . . . *I mustn't forget to buy some bread* . . . 'Bec, tongue studs and cultural meaning. We would love to hear your thoughts on this' . . . *oh dear, oh no, oh what?*

'Umm, tongue studs, well, tongue studs are a way of defining identity, which is one way, um . . . One of the ways young people assert their individuality is by adopting dress codes and body practices that go outside the ah, the ah, cultural norm . . . and body piercing fits this paradigm as relates to youth culture.'

I tailed off, unsure of how successful my total fudging had been. Mr Buckley loved the word paradigm, but I was hoping he wouldn't ask me how this tongue stud stuff related to *A Streetcar Named Desire* because I hadn't got around to reading it yet. In fact I didn't even know where my copy was, possibly under my bed.

Fortunately my Good Luck Goddess intervened and sent Mr Buckley a major sneeze attack. By the time he'd pulled out his big icky-looking handkerchief and done some intensive nose-blowing, he'd forgotten about me, and foolishly requested Gregory Mallory to discuss the relationship between Blanche and Stella in terms of current gender politics. Gregory Mallory looked about as blank as if he'd been asked to produce a ferret from his pocket. Mr Buckley blasted us all for not studying the text thoroughly, and everyone was very glad when it was time to go home. Except that just as we began to pack up our gear, Mr Buckley got his revenge by assigning us a short essay on either gender politics or cultural assumptions as related to *A Streetcar Named Desire*, three pages, to be done by the next day. Damn, bother and blast.

surprises

I stopped off at the supermarket on Jamieson Street and bought a packet of fettuccine, some bacon, a tub of cream, and a lettuce, which I hoped wouldn't squash too much when I shoved it in my backpack. I decided to make pasta carbonara and a salad, with tinned peaches and ice-cream for dessert. I could almost see my mother looking at my purchases in a slightly disapproving manner. 'Too bad,' I said out loud. 'Not everyone has to be a perfect cook, you know, Vera,' I added under my breath, because a man eating an ice-cream outside the supermarket was looking at me strangely.

I started to cycle home and then remembered that I'd forgotten to buy bread, so I had to turn around and go back. By the time I got home I was grumpy.

I stomped into the kitchen and plonked everything on the table. Josh and Bing were nowhere to be seen but their bikes were in the shed and they'd left a trail of milky blobs and cracker crumbs all over the kitchen.

'We're on the computer,' Bing yelled from upstairs.

'You left a big mess down here, you wankers!' I yelled back. No reply. Oh well, let them stay on the computer while I unpack the groceries and sort myself out a bit.

Three messages on the answering machine. I'll check them out in a minute but first I have to go pee. I glance at the clock . . . bloody hell, it's already quarter to five. Soon I'll have to start preparing dinner. Oh no, I suddenly remember that I have not just one but two homework assignments, the Lit one and a long French translation we were given last week, both due in tomorrow. I haven't even begun. The thought is not a happy one. Being in charge sucks. Now I am mother, father, housekeeper and sister all rolled into one, and it's hard work. No point stressing though. I'll just do one thing at a time, I tell myself. One thing at a time.

Just as I came out of the bathroom the phone rang. It was

Jaz, going a million miles an hour, like an ecstatic angel on speed. 'Bec, guess what? Sam rang, which is amazing because it's only Monday. He wants to come to the party, which is so joy. I asked Nick and he's coming for sure. He just headed out for a skate, he said to say hi to Bec, he's going to bring Steve and maybe Pete as well. Pete is gorgeous, he's very quiet but nice. He might be just right for Katherine, or maybe Julia . . . I'll bring vegetarian sushi, will that be okay?'

'Cool,' I said. 'Oh, go away!'

'What?' asked Jaz.

'Sorry, I didn't mean you, Jaz, I was talking to Eggy, Bing's cat. I nearly tripped over him, he's under my feet being a pain because he wants to be fed. I've got to go though, it's the house of chaos here . . . Great about Sam, great about Nick, great about sushi, talk to you tomorrow, okay?'

I unwound the phone cord, which I'd managed to get tangled up in while trying to avoid the cat. 'Get out of my kitchen, Nasty Mr Eggleton. I'll feed you later, that is if I don't decide to throttle you instead.' The cat tried to slide away from me, but I grabbed him and carried him down the hall. I opened the front door, poised to dump Eggleton outside and nip back in before he snuck inside. I was lost in a little daydream about black cats and witches and magic spells, when I heard something odd. The sound of a car coming up the drive.

I glanced up to see a purple Volkswagen Beetle. There was only one person in it and he was getting out. It was Steve!

I was so stunned that I forgot to shut the door. Eggleton raced down the hall towards the kitchen. I swore he gave me a smug smile as he scooted past.

Steve bounded up the steps.

'What are you doing here?' I blurted. It sounded dreadful but it was too late because I'd already said it.

'I was having a skate with Nick. Jaz was there and she told me what happened. I thought I'd swing by, see if you were okay.' Steve was scratching his arm, staring at the ground. I realised he was feeling shy and dorky. How could I have been so rude? But still . . . why has he come? Doesn't he know Saturday night was a big mistake? What am I going to do?'

'Come on in,' I said hastily, trying to look welcoming. 'I didn't mean to be rude. My head is totally bent out of shape right now.'

Steve grinned some more. His eyes were an amazing blue. How come I hadn't noticed that on Saturday? He was wearing totally baggy cargo shorts and a t-shirt that said BEER, SO MUCH MORE THAN JUST A BREAKFAST DRINK. I have to admit he looks really cool.

'Want a cup of coffee?'

'Water would be good.'

We sat down at the kitchen table with our drinks, neither of us sure what to do next.

'Pretty bad, the housekeeper thing,' said Steve, skulling his water.

Just then Bing came thundering down the stairs. 'Who's this?' she demanded.

'A friend of mine. Steve, meet Bing.'

Bing shook his hand. She thought she was cute. She was, sort of.

'I'm starving. What's for dinner, Bec?'

'Pasta. I'm just going to start making it.'

'Hey, Steve, wanna see my animals before dinner?'

He looked at me. I looked at him and shrugged. Not much else I could do.

HOW TO COOK EASY FETTUCCINE CARBONARA À LA BEC

(serves 4)
1 large onion, sliced thinly
4 cloves garlic, peeled and thinly sliced
300 grams of fettuccine
4 rashers of bacon, chopped
half a tub of thickened cream
100 grams of grated parmesan cheese

Fry the onion in a splash of olive oil over a medium heat
until it is soft and golden. Remove the onion from the pan
and fry the bacon until it is nice and crispy. Add the garlic
and fry a tiny bit longer. Meanwhile, cook the fettuccine
in a pot of boiling water until it is al dente, which means

cooked but still firm and chewy, unless you like your pasta a bit soft and gluggy, in which case go for it. Drain the pasta, and while it is still nice and hot, add the fried yummy things and the cream. Swirl it all around and eat at once. You can shove in some other stuff like olives if the spirit moves you. Serve the parmesan separately. There are two sorts of people in this world: those who love parmesan and those who think it should be avoided because it smells like old sneakers.

Steve stayed for dinner. There was no way out of it because Bing had more or less invited him. Josh entertained us with a few facts he'd found on a new website, Steve told Bing lots of stories about gory skate accidents, the pasta tasted creamy and yummy and fine. We drank Milo. I couldn't find any peaches so we ate ice-cream and the last of the Tim Tams. Steve, Josh and Bing did the dishes, combining your actual washing and drying with a frenzy of tea towel flicking. When they had finished the bench was all wet and there were bits of vegetable gunk all over the sink but hey, the job was done.

'Want to read *Harry Potter* with me?' Bing asked Steve.

'Another time, okay? I have to split,' Steve said, looking around for somewhere to hang up the soggy tea towel.

I followed him out to the car. He wasn't as tall and skinny as Nick, but he still had to fold himself up to fit into the driver's seat.

'Thanks for coming over.'

'No worries. Call me if I can do anything.'

'I don't have your number,' I mumbled. It was a million zillion miles from what I'd meant to say. Oh no, now he'd think I liked him. Steve scrabbled round on the floor of the Beetle, found a ball-point, scribbled his number on an old business card. He gave me a goofy thumbs up sign. I smiled like a moron. He drove off into the night.

I should have said that Saturday was all a mistake. But you can't undo kissing someone. I should have told him about the party. But how could I do both? Anyhow, maybe I did like him. I mean I liked him, but not the same way I liked Nick, but perhaps that was just a fantasy, a schoolgirl crush . . .

I was so knackered I couldn't think straight. There was still heaps to be done. I fed Eggleton. Yuck. Tinned cat food had to be one of the most revolting substances on this planet. I dragged myself upstairs, wandered into Bing's room. Her light was off but there was a slice of moonlight illuminating the fish tank. Theodore languidly circled around and around. Not a bad life, being a turtle. No homework. Although you did have to eat dried maggots.

Before I could open my mouth to say goodnight, Bing asked, 'Hey, Bec, is Steve your boyfriend now?'

'No way. For heavens' sake, Bing, just because someone is male, and is also my friend, that does not equal a boyfriend. Now go to sleep.'

'How come he's not your boyfriend? I like him, he's nice.'

'Yeah right, whatever. Go to sleep, okay?'

'Mum and Dad and the monkeys will be home soon,' she mumbled sleepily and tucked down under her doona.

Josh was all snuggled up, his head buried in a book of amazing facts. 'Look at this, Bec.' He offered me a page.

'111,111,111 times 111,111,111 equals 12345678987654321.'

'Wow, pretty cool.'

'And did you know that you can lead a cow upstairs but not down?'

'No, I didn't, but it's time for lights out now. It's late and I've still got a dreaded Lit assignment to do. Goodnight, Josh Bosh.'

I got out smartly so that I wouldn't be stuck there hearing that human beings are the only primates with no pigment in the palms of their hands, or that if you put a raisin in a glass of champagne it rises to the top of the glass and sinks to the bottom over and over again. If only I knew how to channel Josh's brilliance into writing my Lit essay. Amazing facts are all very well but there isn't a lot you can do with an amazing fact except be amazed.

All I wanted to do was crash but there was the small matter of the homework. I searched under my bed and found my black sock, twenty cents and the dusty copy of A Streetcar Named Desire. I tried to do the French translation but I couldn't get a grip. Perhaps some caffeine would help.

I put the kettle on and then I remembered the messages. The

first one was Mrs Dempster. Oh Cripes, I never rang the hospital. Her voice sounded doo-whacky-doo, maybe she was high on pain medication. She asked if we were okay and said I needed to call the social worker at the hospital. Then she repeated the whole thing all over again and got cut off in mid-sentence. The second caller didn't leave a message. There was just a click. I hate that. You always wonder who it was.

All of a sudden the night was alive with Vera's familiar voice.

'Darlings, it's Mum. We made it to New Mexico! Hacienda del Sol is gorgeous, although the cook pours maple syrup over the sausage-cake thingies at breakfast, which tastes dreadful. Anyhow, hope you're out having fun, we'll ring again in a day or two. We miss you lots and lots but it's not long now until we're home. Here's Dad . . .'

Lewis's deep voice echoed in the quiet night kitchen.

'You three would love it here. Taos is wonderful, such a vibrant cultural mix, and the landscape is amazing. Tomorrow we visit an ancient Native American Pueblo site–'

Click. The message cut out.

~~~~

I sat in the darkness and had a little cry. Hearing my parent's voices hit me with a thud. Suddenly I missed them. Quite a bit, really. Mrs Dempster and her accident was starting to feel like a big trauma, even though I had tried to handle it. There was no way I could do my goddamn Lit essay this late at night. I hadn't even read the stupid play. The worst thing of all was the thing about Nick and Steve. How come Nick hadn't called, seeing he knew about the accident and everything? . . . So much for him liking me. And Steve, he was really kind but . . . I was so tired I couldn't think properly. My period was due as well, which always made me feel wonky. Then my special voice cut in, the inner voice that sometimes told me what to do when things were weird and jumbly. 'Go to bed, sugar,' it said. So I did.

terror

I wake up. There's someone outside. I can hear them thumping about in the garden. What's the time? Two-thirty. I must be imagining it. It's only my imagination, right? This is classic. Now I'm inventing night noises, just because it's only us kids here. But I *can* hear someone outside, someone walking on the verandah. Get a grip, Bec. It's just your fear, turning you inside-out. Could be Eggleton, or the wind knocking a branch against a window.

Every horror movie I ever saw is writhing around my brain.

Invisible evil, lurking in the shadows, nameless but deadly.

A lunatic with a knife.

An alien who has no need of a knife, who will suck our brains out as easily as pouring milk.

It's nothing. It's nothing. It's nothing, I pretend. But then

I hear the front door opening and someone turning on a light in the kitchen.

I should ring the police but the phone is in the kitchen. I should climb out the window and somehow get help but I can't leave Bing and Josh. *Jesus Mary Mother of God help me help me.* What am I going to do?

It's too late. Whoever it is, they're coming up the stairs.

There are footsteps sneaking along the hall. In the movies the heroine always screams now but what's the use of that? Who will hear me?

~~~

'Bec?' someone whispers.

'Linda! What are you doing here?'

'The social worker at the hospital rang me. Mrs Dempster is panicking about you lot being alone. I would have come earlier but we had a big crowd at the restaurant, very unusual for a Monday. A group of lady bowlers. Anyway, I came as soon as I could. Sorry I didn't ring, bit hectic really, the veggie order didn't get delivered . . .'

'Oh, Linda, I thought you were a nutter with a knife.'

'Yeah, well, I am really, but I only use it on chicken breasts. You poor baby, everything's okay, go back to sleep now, come on, let me tuck you in.'

~~~

Next morning I woke up early, still half lost in a dream. The harder I tried to catch it the more it slipped away, wispy as cloud, but it left behind a silky trail of boats and blue and sea.

Then I remembered yesterday, and Steve coming over, and the midnight horror show, and Linda turning up. Now I was totally wide awake. Seeing it was so early I might as well have a crack at the essay.

HOW TO FUDGE A LIT ESSAY

First, read the beginning and the ending of the set text.
Next, examine the notes your teacher gave you.
Make up some ideas.
Skim through the text until you find some quotes that vaguely fit your argument.
Use your imagination. Cobble together something in the region of what your teacher expects you to say.
Put in lots of buzz words, like genre, gender and paradigm.
Say a little prayer. Hand it in.

I used to think only girls like Lisa did stuff like this but now I was doing it. I was a natural. It was as easy as anything. I wouldn't get a brilliant mark but desperate times called for desperate measures. Thank goodness for Lewis's computer. My fingers plunked the keys like clumsy grasshoppers but by eight o'clock I had churned out something halfway decent, if you didn't think too hard about the finer points of my argument, which was that the sister relationship had both positive and negative aspects in terms of gender politics. That's what I love about Lit theory. You can say absolutely any old bulldust as long as you back it up with lots of quotes.

Linda made pancakes for breakfast, and gave us money to buy our lunches, which was choice. School was pretty boring. Mrs Tait gave a lunchtime detention to everyone who hadn't done their translation, so I didn't get to catch up with my friends. I could have got out of it, with my radically cool My-Parents-Are-Away-&-Our-Housekeeper-Fell-Down-A-Hole excuse, but to tell the truth I was glad to have some time out. It was easier to do the translation than to think about Nick, Steve, the party, Katherine's love life, and other catastrophes of modern day living.

On the way home I met Josh and Bing and we raced, pedalling like lunatics. I would have won except Bing got a bindi-eye in her tyre, so we called it a truce. There was no sign of Linda but she'd left us a note and a bag of Hershey Kisses. PREPARE FOR MORE SURPRISES it said in fancy green scribble. Good old Lin.

We were in the shed, mucking around trying to work out how to use the puncture kit, when we heard a car coming up the drive.

'Probably your boyfriend,' said Bing.

'Doubt it,' I answered, and then stopped still. How come I hadn't said, he isn't my boyfriend? What was even stranger was that I was half hoping it *was* Steve.

However, it was not a purple Volkswagen driven by a wild-haired boy with a goofy smile.

It was an ambulance.

The driver jumped out, an Annie-Lennox look-alike with short bleached hair. She opened the back door and Mrs Dempster slowly emerged, leg encased in a huge plaster. She was still clutching her rainbow raffia handbag. Before I had time to say hello she launched into a waterfall of words.

'Bec, how are you, is everything all right? I've been so worried about you. The fracture isn't as bad as they first thought, thank goodness. I'll be in plaster for ages but at least your parents won't have to get someone else in. I think we can manage for a week until they get back, don't you?'

'We're fine.' Josh and Bing joined me on the front step.

'Oh goodie, you're back, can I sign your cast?' Bing asked.

Josh was smiling, and I must admit it was sort of a relief that Mrs Dempster was home, except for two things. Was I still in the shit? What about the party?

'Okay, let's get the patient inside,' said Annie Lennox. Mrs Dempster clumped down the hall, and settled herself on the big comfy couch in the living room.

'Whew!' she said.

'Well, I'll be off,' said the blond woman. 'You've got your pain medication, and the hospital will arrange transport for your first check-up. You should get a letter in the next few days. Take it easy, won't you? Bye for now.'

'I'll start the dinner,' I said.

'Can you manage, Bec? I'm probably not going to be much use to anyone for a day or two, I'm still a bit groggy from the pain pills.'

'Sure, no worries. Like a cup of tea?'

'That would be lovely, dear.' Mrs D smiled and closed her eyes. 'I probably just need to rest here for a while. Bing, how about after dinner you get the felt-tip pens and do a lovely drawing for me to brighten up this ghastly white plaster.'

When we had eaten Mrs Dempster dozed off in her chair while Josh and Bing set to work on her leg. Red flowers, green leaves, purple birds, yellow suns, blue clouds and orange hearts. Bing's drawings are as bright and exuberant as she is. Josh painstakingly created a zoo of tiny black creatures, strange friendly looking creatures with wings and beaks and curly tails.

'That's brilliant, you guys. But hey, it's nine o'clock, so come on, off to bed.'

Mrs Dempster managed the stairs by going up backwards on her bottom, dragging her cumbersome, colourful leg behind her.

'Will you be okay, Mrs D?' I asked, when she'd made it into the bedroom and flopped herself down on the bed.

'I'll be fine. I'm going to sleep like a log.'

'Mrs D?'

'Mmmm?'

'I'm sorry about the other night. We ended up staying at another friend's house. I should have told you, it's just that it was a guy's house, and I thought you'd say no, but it was okay, his mother was there, we slept in the shed . . .' I realised I was blathering, so I stopped.

'I need to be able to trust you, Bec . . . and you might have a go at trusting me a bit more. I was young once, too, you know. Look, I know you haven't found it easy having me around instead of your parents. Why don't we make a fresh start, okay?'

'Cool,' I said.

'Turn out the light, there's a good girl. I can hear the angels calling me.'

I made for the safety of my room. Brilliant. I was out of Deep Shitsville. There was still the matter of the party though, but there was no way I could ask about that tonight. I lay on my bed giggling, remembering the Jack Kerouac saying that Mr Buckley told us: 'Walking on water wasn't built in a day.'

~~~~

In the morning Mrs Dempster was clumping around the kitchen like a clumsy but cheerful hippopotamus.

'Think I'll ring Foodland and see if they deliver,' she said, munching her toast.

'Good plan,' I replied. I really wanted to ask about Saturday night but I needed a strategy first. What if she said no? Or worse, what if she said *yes*? There was no way we could have a party with her there. I needed time to think. I scooted through my cereal, whacked together a cheese and Vegemite sandwich. Josh and Bing weren't ready but I wasn't going to wait. If they were late it was no big deal, but if I was late I'd get a late pass. 'Gotta go, see you after school.' I grabbed an apple, which would have to do instead of cleaning my teeth, and dashed out the door.

~~~

'This is tragic,' said Katherine, when lunchtime finally came.

'Bummer,' said Lisa.

Jaz and Julia said nothing. We all sat there looking glum for a while.

'I mean it's good that Mrs Dempster's leg is okay but Saturday night was going to be so cool,' I said after a while, more for something to say than for any other reason. SBO, we call it in our family, Stating the Blooming Obvious.

More glum silence.

'I thought the party was definite,' Jaz said at last. 'I mean, I already asked Sam, and Nick and Steve and Pete were definitely coming.'

'Yeah,' Lisa added, 'my mother even said it would be okay if I came—a miracle considering *her* head-space right now.'

'Isn't there *any* way?' Julia piped up. 'Like what about if you asked Mrs D and she said yes and she agreed to go somewhere for the night?'

'Yeah, and pigs might fly,' I replied. My sandwich tasted dry and revolting. I should have put lettuce in it or something. 'I mean, I can ask her, I guess.'

'Yeah, at least ask her. It's worth a shot,' Katherine piped up hopefully.

The others said nothing but I could feel their expectations on me, as heavy as a cloak of iron.

~~~

I spent the last half of lunchtime making a hash of my flute lesson. I thought the day couldn't get much worse but I was wrong. Mr Buckley decided to make people read their essays aloud and, wouldn't you just know it, I was one of the lucky ones. Reading mine out made me very conscious of what a rush job it was, but I read it in a loud confident voice. Sometimes brazening it out is all you can do.

'Interesting,' said Mr Buckley. 'Any comments, class?'

I stared hard at Gregory Mallory, daring him with eyes of poison to say a thing, and willing Mr Buckley to choose Gregory next if he dared to open his mouth. I wondered what my horoscope would say for this week.

'Jupiter, the planet of activity, and Saturn,
the planet of difficulty and obstruction, are in
your sign this week, Leo. Prepare for a major
meltdown. You would be best advised to hide under
your doona with a good book until the planets
have decided to behave themselves.'

~~~

Last class of the day was Art.

'Self-portraits,' Miss Bell said when we were all more or less quiet. 'How do you see yourself?' she began and started one of her raves.

I like Miss Bell. Short black hair, short black skirts, black Doc Martens, talkative, slightly batty. She's actually a textile artist. I guess she only teaches because making wonderful fabrics doesn't pay her rent. Her class is fun because it's last thing in the day and it isn't a core subject. Usually Miss Bell just raves on for a while and no one takes much notice. Then we paint or draw something and then we go home.

'Who are you? Are you a fixed entity or are you, as Walt Whitman so beautifully described it, "a multitude"? How do you choose to represent yourself?'

Miss Bell was getting passionate now. Gregory Mallory was scratching his leg with a paint brush and staring out the window but I was interested. Lately I felt as though whoever I once was had left town, leaving only a confusing tumble of emotions in her place. I wasn't the sensible Bec any more but I wasn't a wild new Bec either. I didn't know who I was.

'We're going to do an exercise. Pick a partner. Centre yourselves, and then make eye contact. One person asks the question 'who are you?' over and over again and the other one answers, each time in a different way. Be playful, have a bit of fun. It's a great way to break through stale fixed ideas of yourself into a more creative space. Keep at it until I tell you to swap over.'

I looked around for a partner. None of my friends were in this class. I didn't really know anyone except Gregory Mallory. There was no way I would do anything at all with him so I was glad when I saw him pair up with Brian Murchison. Now everyone except me had a partner.

'Oh, odd numbers, come on, Bec, you can work with me. Righty-ho class, steady up. Decide who's going to be the first one to ask the question, centre yourselves and begin.'

I took a deep breath. Tried not to feel silly. Tried to look Miss Bell in the eyes instead of staring at her dangly earrings or her slightly smudgy crimson lipstick.

Who are you?
Bec.
Who are you?
Vera's daughter.
Who are you?
The older sister.
Who are you?
Tired.
Who are you?
A palm tree.
Who are you?
Confused.

Who are you?

Henna Queen.

Who are you?

Hungry.

Who are you?

Peach milk-shake.

Who are you?

Tangled up in blue.

Who are you?

Love sick.

Who are you?

A broken skateboard.

Who are you?

Purple roses.

Who are you?

Tumbling waves.

Who are you?

Fifteen.

Who are you?

Sky cloud.

Who are you?

Everything.

Who are you?

I was running out of answers. I paused, trying to think of something, anything. Miss Bell grinned and left the question hanging in the air. She clapped her hands.

'Okay, swap over, class,' she ordered.

'I'm a hot sausage,' I heard Gregory Mallory say.

Brian Murchison brayed like a donkey on laughing gas. God, those two were a couple of dags.

'I'm going to pike on this one, Bec,' said Miss Bell. 'My personality is way too evil and complex to reveal to an innocent girl like you. Come on, give me a hand to get the gear out. It's mixed media today, I'll get the paints and you get the pastels, one set for each table. I've already put the inks out.'

As I laid out the boxes of dusty pastels, I couldn't help overhearing some of the answers. They were classic. Brian Murchison's were unfit for human ears. Darren Sweeney, who is the largest boy in the school, said 'don't know' a lot and then hit upon the idea of answering with different foods, like roast chicken with gravy and mashed potatoes. Sara Atkinson, who is rather sappy, was an angel with glittery wings, a soft kitten, and a rainbow. Freud would have had a field day with us.

'So, a self portrait. Go for it, guys,' urged Miss Bell, when the question game was over. 'Don't think too hard, just let the materials speak to you, and respond to the question 'who am I?' in any way you choose, either literally or in an abstract way.' She put on a tape of smooth jazz, and busied herself wrapping messy lumps of clay in damp hessian.

I sat at my favourite bench, the small one next to the window. No one came and sat beside me. I stared at the clean white sheet of paper. So fresh. So inviting. So daunting.

Always the moment of hesitation, just before beginning. Always the doubt, the tiny fear, the not knowing. With black ink and a fine pen I drew a mermaid. I drew a tail of tiny glistening scales. I drew hair that swirled and whirled and became the swirly whirly ocean.

I wet the paintbrush, dipped it in blue, in pink, in turquoise.

Who am I?

I am a mermaid. I want to swim for ever in a sea of colours.

popping the question

I cycled home as fast as I could. I had to talk to Mrs Dempster before I lost my nerve. You can do it, Bec. I crossed my fingers in case it would help. Maybe it sounds crazy but I felt really good that afternoon. Painting the mermaid had made me brave.

Mrs D was tucked up on the couch, surrounded by a pile of magazines. 'This is the life, maybe I should break my leg more often. How was your day?'

'Okay, fine. We had Art. It was fun. But . . . the thing is . . . I need to talk to you about something important.'

'What's up?'

I didn't know where to begin so I just blurted it out. That I was glad she was back but that I was really freaked out because, well, because my friends and I had arranged a bit of a party for Saturday night.

'A bit of a party, mmm. So how big are we talking here?' Mrs D asked when I had finished. I was too nervous to look at her but at least she hadn't said no. Yet.

'Um, well, me and Jaz and Katherine and Lisa and Julia, that's five, and Jaz's brother, Nick, that's six, and Pete and Steve, his two friends, that's eight, and Jeremy, who works at the burger bar with Lisa, that makes nine altogether. Oh, and Sam, he's a friend of Jaz's. So that makes ten. Everyone is going to bring some food and we'll just hang out and play some music. I thought maybe Bing could stay over at Megan's house and Josh, well, umm, I wasn't sure about Josh . . .' I tailed off. I held my breath and prayed to The Goddess of Happy Miracles. Please, please, please.

When you are waiting for something, time can stretch out very long. It took Mrs D about twenty seconds to answer but it felt like for ever. I stared at the rose pattern on the rug, and kept praying.

'Well, I don't see why not. A party would be fun for you and your friends. As long as it is a small affair, I don't think your parents would mind. I'm so sorry you've had to cope with my accident, Bec, I feel dreadful about that. I should have phoned the evening it happened but I was so doped up on morphine, all I remember is floating in and out of sleep, and a nurse coming in about four times to ask me if I had passed a bowel movement. It gave me the giggles, actually, at the time. I must have been very out of it because even wearing that dreadful hospital nightgown didn't bother me. There's something to be said for legal drugs, isn't there?'

I looked at Mrs D. She was smiling. Just for a second I saw the young living-in-London-having-a-ball person, and then we were back to the present moment and she was Mrs D again.

I picked at my fingernail, concentrating on picking a tiny dry bit of hangnail off without pulling too hard and making it sore. There was one more tricky bit still to go.

'The thing is . . .' I stopped, trying to think of a polite way to say it. There wasn't one. 'The thing is, I was sort of hoping to have no adults . . .'

'I thought you might be hoping that. I remember how mortified I was when I was sixteen and my father wanted to pick me up outside a dance. I probably hurt his feelings terribly, insisted he park three streets away and wait for me in the car. Moving away from adults, into your own world, all part of growing up. Necessary, but bloody painful. How's this for a good idea? Patrick rang up today, just to see how things were going. He flies back from Broome on Friday, and he kept asking if there was anything he could do to help. Why don't Josh and I go down to the cottage on Saturday night? I'm sure Patrick would love to have us, and Bing can sleep over at Megan's.'

'Mrs D, you are an angel of the first degree.' I was so happy I gave her a clumsy sort of a hug. It's hard to hug someone when they're sitting down but I did it anyway.

'What time would you come home?' I blurted. I felt all speedy and over-excited. My party was really going to happen.

'How about midnight? Josh can have a snooze on the couch when he gets tired and I'll ask Patrick if he minds dropping us home.'

'Mrs D, this is so cool.' I had been secretly hoping she'd say they would stay over so we could kick on all night, but I figured I should quit while I was ahead. 'I think I'll go and call my friends. Can I get you something?'

'A cup of tea would be lovely, dear. Nice and strong with a splosh of honey. I can hear Josh and Bing putting their bikes in the shed, could you sort them out? . . . I got some groceries delivered so there's plenty of snacky things.'

I made the tea, pointed Josh and Bing at the juice and crackers, and headed upstairs with the phone. First I called Lisa. She was rapt.

'Is it okay if Tom comes, too?' she asked. 'He's an Engineering student friend of Jeremy's. I haven't met him but Jeremy had an arrangement to go clubbing with him or something on Saturday, so he kind of doesn't want to let him down.'

'Sure,' I said, casually. 'The more the merrier.'

Lisa had to do a Final Total Homework Blitz, so we signed off.

You had to admire Lisa's Blitz Method. Lisa was well known for her Blitz Method, which was to ignore all homework until it was way overdue, then lock herself in her room with a pot of coffee and much crunchy junk food, and not come out until her assignments were done. This could mean that she began at four in the afternoon and kept going until two or three in the morning. The annoying thing was that she always pushed the envelope to the max but she got the best mark for everything when she finally handed her stuff in. It drove the teachers insane.

Anyhow, next I rang Julia. Katherine was there, too. Jools said she'd bring chips and dips, and try to score a bottle of champagne. Katherine said she'd make her special chocolate beetroot cake, with the sexy buttery chocolate icing. 'Brilliant,' I said. I asked Julia about borrowing something to wear, she said no worries, I could come over after school any day to look at her clothes. 'I might even buy a new outfit,' I said suddenly. I had just remembered my dressing gown pocket, in which there was four hundred and thirty-two dollars and fifteen cents, approximately. Amazing that I kept forgetting about it, but the coloured yarn extravaganza that was my life was so tangled and whizzy that even important things were easy to forget. Each time I remembered the money it was a new surprise, like winning all over again.

'We could go into town on Thursday after school, I could help you look. I'm going in anyway to pick up this seriously gorgeous fabric that I've got on layby. They've got some stunning dresses at Voodoo Doll we could check out.'

'That would be magic, Jools.'

I hoped Katherine wouldn't be upset about it. She can get a bit thingy about being left out. Maybe we could all meet up, except that shopping was much harder when you had five opinions. We tended to lose focus when we tried to shop in a group. Once I bought a skirt at Subway DC that didn't fit me properly because my friends insisted I looked hell-cute. Shopping with one other person was definitely safer.

'Gotta ring Jaz and tell her. See you guys, bye.'

I pressed the Jaz button on my touch phone. Lewis had shown me how to program it. It was cool.

'Hi, is Jaz there?' I asked. I wasn't concentrating properly as I was taking my school uniform off at the time. Underwear is by far the most comfortable talking-on-the-phone outfit.

'She's out. I can get her to phone you though. Or you could talk to me for a while instead, which would be even better.'

jelly knees

I know it's a cliché but now I know where the cliché came from. My knees actually did get a sort of wobbly jelly feel when I heard that voice, even though by then I was sprawled out on my bed in my green satin bra and boxers, lying on my back with my legs stretched halfway up the wall, which is one of my most comfortable talking-on-the-phone positions.

'Hi, Nick.' It was a pretty basic start to a conversation but for the first few seconds I was in a space void and couldn't think properly. Luckily, out of the thin blue air, words came tumbling. 'The party, it's on. Mrs D is going out, only till midnight unfortunately, but at least she agreed to the party. So you can tell your friends to come on by.'

I felt really shy about the thought of actually seeing Nick again. I didn't want him to know how all-over-the-place I was feeling, or blurt out anything dumb. 'How's Uni going?' I asked, to fill the gap.

Twenty-seven minutes later Mrs Dempster called me for dinner so I said goodbye and hung up the phone. I don't know how I got down the stairs. I definitely did not walk down. I think I sort of floated or flew or something.

I tucked into a big helping of chicken and salad.

'Nick, Jaz's brother, has to do a garden design project for Uni, and the place he was going to do fell through, so I said he could take a look at our patio. He's coming over later, to look at it, about eight o'clock, if he can get his dad's car. Is that okay?'

'No harm in him coming over,' said Mrs D. 'That patio is a real disaster, that's for sure. Now, about Saturday, Josh and I are going to have a nice night down at Patrick's place, and we're going to ring Mrs Murphy after tea to arrange a sleepover, aren't we, Bing?'

'Yeah, but whoa, Bec's got a boy coming over. Romance city, call Channel Nine,' yelled Bing, triumphantly.

'God, Bing, shut up! He's only coming over to see the garden,' I said, but I was blushing. Fortunately Josh started prattling on about the Hanging Gardens of Babylon. He would have kept going until he'd described the other six wonders of the world as well if Mrs Dempster hadn't made him and Bing go and do the dishes.

I went upstairs and put on my old blue dress, the soft one with red roses on it. It was getting a bit raggedy and had a small hole near the hem but it was still my favourite. I pinned my fringe back with two glittery clips but it looked really dorky so I took them out again. I tried to do my homework but I didn't have a snowflake's chance in hell of concentrating, so I gave up and went downstairs. Bing and Josh were outside, playing something noisy, and Mrs D was propped on the sofa, doing embroidery. Skeins of cotton were lined up on the arm of the sofa beside her: sea-rose red, rich purple, burnt orange, electric green, sunflower yellow. A row of neat and tidy colours. Not a messy, complicated wriggle like life.

'What are you making?' I plonked down in Lewis's green armchair and tried to sit still. It was twenty to eight and I was in a state of total panic.

'I'm not crash-hot at embroidery actually, but I find it very relaxing. One day these squares will become a quilt. I just embroider whatever takes my fancy. I'm working on a flower right now. I thought it was a rose but it seems to be turning into a peony.'

'Cool,' I said. Mrs D could have said she had a passion for murdering small furry animals and I wouldn't have known the difference. I hopped up, went into the kitchen, peered in the fridge, went back into the lounge. 'Mrs D,' I blurted. 'Is it always like this, liking someone, I mean?'

'Like what, exactly?'

'Like, scary and embarrassing and awful.'

'Tell me about awful.'

I glanced at Mrs D. She looked all calm and friendly, so even though I was feeling silly I kept at it. 'Awful like, what if a guy doesn't like me the same way I like him? Awful like not knowing what's going to happen, awful like I look in the mirror and I look crappy, awful like I feel . . . I just feel . . . dumb and ugly and ordinary.'

Sometimes you don't know you feel something until you say it. Now I had said it I felt even more dumb, so I stared at the carpet. I pretended I was safe and far away, a white bird soaring over ocean.

'Oh, Bec, you funny girl. I do know how you feel, though. Love is one of the great mysteries, one of the strangest journeys you're ever going to take. Yes, what you're experiencing is totally normal, and yes, it is scary, but it's wonderful too. The main thing is to enjoy it, the sheer deliciousness of it, which is somehow inseparable from the ghastly bits, like the trepidation and the not knowing what comes next. If there were anything I could give you it would be the gift of knowing how lovely you are, how beautiful and special. No one but you can give yourself that gift, though, and I should know, I've spent a lifetime trying. But you're not ordinary, Bec. No one is ordinary.'

God, life is weird. I remembered how in the beginning I had thought Mrs D was dreary, and now there she was on the sofa, glowing and smiling at me like some kind of amazing wise woman. Saint Dawn of the Bung Leg and the Big Red Hands and the Very Kind Heart. I didn't know what to say, so I didn't say anything. I just smiled back, across far more distance than a lounge room. I could tell by her eyes that Mrs D had heard me.

Then I went out to join Bing and Josh in the garden. We played our own made-up game, called Scramble. It's sort of like Chasey and sort of like Statues, and it involves some standing in ridiculous poses, plenty of running and yelling, and a fair bit of laughing and tickling. And maybe it looked a bit silly when Nick and Steve drove up in the purple Beetle, but it can't have looked that silly, because they joined in as well.

~~~

Midnight. I lay awake in the dark. I couldn't sleep. I liked them both. What was going to happen at the party?

wednesday at school

The idea that teenagers are unmotivated is definitely false. Jaz and Lisa and Katherine and Julia and I achieved huge amounts when we chose to.

At lunchtime, sprawled in the shade of the gum tree at the far end of the hockey field, fuelled by Coffee Chill and rising excitement, we discussed exactly which guys were coming to the party. Nick, Sam, Steve, Pete, Jeremy, Tom. Six guys, five girls, the perfect ratio.

'Not that we're all going to pair up or anything but who knows what the night will bring?' I said lightly.

Jaz glanced at me strangely, or perhaps I imagined it. Katherine tried to find out the maximum amount of information about Steve, Pete, Jeremy and Tom. The Tom part was hard because no one had actually met him. Jaz said Pete was nice, a bit of a dreamer, sandy hair, another skate maniac. Julia and Lisa acted too cool to care, but if you don't mind me saying so they were listening quite intently. We discussed at length what Katherine should wear. Her turquoise dress was voted Outfit Most Likely to Succeed. 'Don't wear anything with a label,' said Julia, The Style Queen. 'No Stussy Mussy, no Nikey Crikey.'

Next, should Jaz metamorphose from post-box red to neon blue? Nah, we all thought the red totally suited her. Drugs and alcohol? Lisa enquired. I thought she was kidding but I wasn't sure so I didn't say anything. Julia had already scored the champagne and the guys would probably bring some beer or something. Food, under control. Jaz, vegetarian sushi. Katherine, chocolate beetroot cake. Julia, chips and dips but really nice ones, not horrible French onion or anything. Smoked salmon pâté and Pringles, maybe.

'Mine's a surprise. Leave it with me, girls,' said Lisa.

We went over the music one more time. Red Hot Chilli Peppers, Tea Party, Sofa King, Blink 182, The Super Furry Animals From Wales. The new Killing Heidi album. Another slight disagreement over Greatest Hits of the Seventies. Jaz said Nick will bring some tunes too. Incense and tea-light candles, for atmosphere? I'll buy them in town on Thursday when Julia and I go shopping. No need, Jaz has some, she'll bring them to school tomorrow. Cool. So, it's all happening, it's party a-go-go. It's going to be hell-fun.

'Guess what, Nick and Steve came over last night.' I casually drop my bombshell. 'Nick has to do a garden for his Uni assignment and he's going to be transforming our crappy patio . . .'

'Into what?' Lisa asks.

'He's not sure yet. He just measured it and wandered around looking thoughtful.' I ignore her sarcasm. I find that's the best way to go with Lisa sometimes.

'Nick *and* Steve. Wow and double wow,' said Katherine.

'Yeah,' I say, just as the siren squawks, saving me from questions to which I have no answers.

~~~

Major miracle. I got seventy-eight percent for my Lit essay on *A Streetcar Named Desire*. The forces of good and evil on the planet are then balanced by the fact that I got into major trouble at my flute lesson.

'Bec, you're not doing any practice at all, are you?' whined Mr Callan, my poor long-suffering flute teacher.

'No, not really,' I replied.

'Well, it is absolutely no use attempting to learn an instrument if you won't do the necessary practice.' Mr Callan looked both grumpy and smug. He thought he had played the absolute last card but he hadn't.

'I'm going to give up flute and take up skateboarding instead,' I said cheerily.

'I imagine you'll live to regret that, Bec,' Mr Callan sniffed.

'Maybe,' I answered, and left the room with as much dignity as I could manage, given that I'd been ratting around on the floor because I'd dropped my flute-cleaning cloth under the desk. I knew I should feel guilty about my current lack of interest in the flute but I felt just fine.

strange times

After school on Thursday, Julia and I caught the bus to town. We fuelled up with a burger and a coke, then picked up her fabric: three metres of stretchy black lace.

'I'm going to make a witch dress,' she laughed, as we walked down the street, arm in arm. It was pretty spooky because right then we glanced up to find we were in front of a magic shop. CELESTIAL VISION said the sign, in gothic lettering. SPELLS: WE HAVE THE STUFF THEY ARE MADE OF. RARE HERBS AND OILS. RITUAL IMPLEMENTS. MAGICAL JEWELLERY. CHARMS. DIVINATION TOOLS. TAROT CARDS. The window was crammed with crystals and stickers and books and fairy wands. Julia and I didn't have to check with each other. We just went in.

'Yes, girls, what can I do for you?' A voice boomed out from behind the counter. I looked and saw a mountain of a woman, with short purple-streaked hair and gypsy earrings: a silver moon and a silver star. She wore a purple kaftan and her fingers were thick with rings.

'Just looking,' said Julia. 'Do you have any magic love spells?' I asked, at the same time. Our voices collided but they didn't cancel each other out. Each seemed to echo around the darkened cavern of the shop.

The woman ignored Julia. 'Have you ever done magic before?' she asked, looking at me intently. Her eyes were a very deep blue.

'No.'

'You have to be careful with magic, you know.'

'Right,' I agreed politely. She didn't say anything else, just kept staring at me with her ocean eyes. I didn't know what else to say, so I smiled at her and went over to see what Julia was doing. She was looking at a statue of a little dragon, a friendly dragon, that had tiny green scales, a pink belly and blue wings. It stood erect, holding a golden orb.

'Cute,' said Julia, handing the dragon to me. I was just about to turn it over to see if it had a price on the bottom when mountain woman said 'five dollars', which was pretty amazing really as we were in a far corner of the shop with our backs to her.

'I'll buy it for you,' I said to Julia. 'As payment for your fashion consultancy.'

Julia grinned.

When I reached the counter I put the dragon down and began scruffling around for my purse. It was in there somewhere, under all the junk at the bottom of my backpack.

'Ten dollars,' said the woman. 'Five for the dragon and five for the love spell,' she continued, before I had a chance to say anything. She tucked the dragon into a dark blue paper bag patterned with gold stars, along with a scroll of red paper, tied with a white ribbon.

'Thank you,' I said.

'You're welcome.'

I'm not sure if it was my imagination, because it was kind of dark in there, but I think the woman winked at me, like a sign, a reminder to take care with the magic.

'That was weird, wasn't it?' I asked, when we were back on the sunny street.

'Yeah, well, cranks and nutters. Did you see that sticker, it was a classic.'

'Which one? MY OTHER CAR IS A BROOMSTICK?'

'Nah, that one's good but my personal favourite is I DO WHATEVER MY RICE CRISPIES TELL ME TO.'

~~~

We wandered along King Street, where the ultra-hip shops are. Hanging in the window of Angels and Insects was a dress. Rose chiffon, cut on the cross, with a petticoat of slinky dark pink satin. I tried it on.

'What do you think?'

'Absolutely *yes*.'

'You reckon?'

'It's stunning. How much is it?'

'A hundred and thirty.'

'It's worth it. Beautifully made and it looks gorgeous on you.'

'Yeah.'

Julia drifted off to check out the beaded cardigans. I looked at myself in the mirror once more. Slowly I took off the dress.

'Let's go.'

'What about the dress?'

I didn't reply. The shop assistant was giving me the evil eye. She actually resembled an insect—a preying mantis—tall and skinny, with a tongue stud and green hair. Back on the street Julia looked quizzical.

'The dress wasn't me,' I mumbled. Julia's quizzical look remained. 'It was . . . it was too nice, too pretty, too predictable.'

Julia shrugged. 'Okay. Let's keep looking.'

'Nah, why don't we go to New Zealand Natural? I can't be bothered doing any more shopping right now.'

'Thanks for the dragon,' said Julia cheerfully, as we slurped our yoghurt cones. 'Now, give me a look at the magic love spell.'

'No way. I can't let just any old person see the spell, lest we are both cursed for ever and turn into two slimy toads.'

'I'm not just "any old person", and you're full of . . .' Julia said. 'Hey, Bec, over there, look, Gregory Mallory, and get this, he's with Sara Atkinson!'

What a sight. Goofy old Gregory, with his bum hanging out of his cargo pants, trying to look cool with just the right amount of satin boxer shorts showing. Arm in arm with flaky Sara. They hadn't noticed us, they were busy looking in the window of a music store.

'Wonders will never cease,' said Julia.

'Cupid on acid,' I replied. 'Nah, let's be nice, they look really sweet and happy,' I continued, trying to undo my bitchiness.

Julia grimaced. 'Yeah, right. Yikes, look at the time. If I run I'll get the six-thirty. You coming?'

'Nah, might look around a bit. See ya.'

~~~

I finished my cone and headed down Hay Street towards the mall. I didn't feel like hurrying. In Down to Earth I looked at the travel books, daydreaming about Turkey and India, exotic places of spice and sun. I bought a card, a photograph of a strange dark-eyed woman inscribed with the words 'Gypsy Queen Card Reader'. I was glad I hadn't bought the dress. The old Bec would have.

On the train I took out the blue paper bag dusted with golden stars. Seeing Goofy Boy and Marshmallow Girl had been a stroke of luck. It meant I didn't have to share my magic spell with Julia. You have to be careful with magic. Gently, I unrolled the red scroll.

A SPELL TO MAKE SOMEONE LOVE YOU

Choose your night with care. The best night is the full moon in Libra. Libra is the astrological sign for relationships; the full moon is a time of power and wholeness. If this is not possible, choose a Friday, as Friday is ruled by Venus, and Venus is the Planet of Love. A crescent moon is also auspicious; the crescent moon is a time of new beginnings.

Gather petals from seven red roses. The rose is associated with Venus, and with romantic love. Take seven white candles. Seven for luck, white for purity. Perform the spell outdoors, beneath a tree, or beside the ocean, in order to harness the power of the natural elements.

Take seven deep breaths. Visualise the person whose love you desire. Using a natural object such as a twig, draw a seven-pointed star on the earth or sand. Arrange the candles at the point of each star. Scatter the rose petals between them.

Light the candles, using only one match. Say these words three times: 'I invoke the heavenly powers to ensure that the one I love will return my affection'. Let the candles burn until they extinguish themselves, and bury the stubs where no eye can see them.

While making this spell you must hold your heart open with joy and kindness so that the enchantment will truly work.

the day before the party

I woke up feeling as excited as a badger on speed. Tried to convince Mrs D that I needed to take the day off school.

'I don't feel very well, I have to cook something, I have to tidy my room, *please*?' I begged, but she had made up her mind. 'You can do all that tomorrow, Bec. You can't fool me, you look a picture of radiant health. Come on, get dressed.'

School was tediously boring. We went over the party plans one last time. Everyone was coming, the travel arrangements were sweet.

'Here's candles and incense and *dah dah*, two purple paper lanterns,' said Jaz.

'Cool,' I said. But I didn't feel in the least bit cool. All of a sudden having a party at my house seemed like a very dumb idea. What if it was boring? What if everyone just sat around and stared at each other? What if Nick decided that Julia was his type of girl?

I didn't share any of my cobwebby fears with my friends. I just lay on my back under the gum tree, imagining I was a pink and grey galah, who only had to peck at seeds and squawk a lot and fly all over the place. Luckily the conversation moved away from the party arrangements into a spectacular mini-drama of another kind. Katherine was really upset because Damian hadn't answered her last three emails.

'It's over, totally over, and I never even met him,' she exclaimed, in her usual melodramatic manner.

'By Monday you'll be madly in love with Tom, Pete and Steve, and they'll all be madly in love with you,' said Lisa, drily.

Jaz giggled. Katherine looked hurt. I pretended to be asleep to avoid being on anyone's side. Julia checked her eyebrows in her pocket mirror and smudged on some lip gloss. It was just another lunchtime at Eastern Hills Senior High.

When I got home from school, Bing and Josh were in the kitchen with Mrs D. Mr Patrick was there too.

'Hey, Mr Patrick, how was Broome?' I asked. Mrs D was calling him Pat now, but I couldn't get past the Mr bit somehow, although he did look sort of younger and more lively that day, in a colourful shirt and corduroy trousers. Down at the cottage he always wore grotty old work gear.

'Wonderful. I had a fascinating—'

'Look, Bec,' Bing butted in. 'A parcel! From Mum and Dad. Mrs D said we had to wait till you got home to open it, cos it's addressed to all of us.'

Josh hacked away at the heavy duty masking tape with his Swiss army knife, refusing to be rushed. Vera has a reputation for wrapping things securely and she'd outdone herself this time. After what seemed like an eternity the parcel was open, revealing three exciting lumpy packets wrapped in tissue. A green one for me, a purple one for Josh and a red one for Bing.

'Look what I got!' yelled Bing, ripping the red tissue off and chucking it everywhere. 'Two packets of sea monkeys, and a t-shirt with a tiger cub on it, and a whole heap of lollies, Hershey Kisses and Rice Krispie Snacks and all different sorts of bubble gum.'

Josh folded the purple paper up into a neat square. His face widened into a smile as he examined a small black object.

'What is it, Josh Bosh?'

'A pocket organiser. We saw them at the airport, remember? It converts from English into five languages and it does all sorts of currencies and everything,' said Josh with delight.

'What's in yours? Bec. Come on, what'd you get?' Bing gabbled, her mouth full of chocolate. I unwrapped slowly. The green tissue paper felt smooth and delicious beneath my fingers.

'Oh, *wow*, beautiful art things.'

'Let me see,' Bing insisted.

'Hang on, you yahoo.' I wanted to savour each gorgeous thing: paper marbled with pink and blue, silver and gold pens, postcards of paintings by Gauguin and Matisse and artists I'd never heard of.

'Poor Mrs D, she didn't get anything,' Bing said.

'Good time to give her this then.' Mr Patrick coughed slightly and took a small square box from his pocket. It was wrapped in tissue paper, too, black and crinkly. 'For you, Dawn. With much affection.'

'Give us a look, what is it?'

'Bing, get some water and do the sea monkey thing, for goodness' sake,' I ordered. My sister poked her tongue out at me and headed for the laundry, redeeming herself slightly by offering Mr Patrick one of her Rice Krispie Snacks.

Mrs D didn't say anything at first, she just looked fragile, as if she might cry. Carefully she took the black pearl earrings out of the velvet box and clipped them on. The pearls were arranged in a flower shape, dark and gleaming and elegant. 'Thank you.' Mr Patrick smiled. 'I think I'll put the kettle on,' said Mrs D.

'Good plan, sweetie,' said Mr Patrick.

Sweetie, if you please. Time to get out of there before it turned into honey-bun and lambkins.

~~~

I went up to my room with a cup of coffee, two bits of raisin toast and a whole pile of cookbooks. Goat's cheese tart with tomato? No way. Anyone who actually ate smelly old goat's cheese had rocks in their head. Toasted flat-bread with mozzarella, avocado and garlic sounded yummy but it was quite fiddly, and I didn't want to be in the kitchen doing stuff while the party was on. Crab and sweet potato fritters? Nah, you had to serve them hot, so that would be a hassle. How about tomato, basil and onion muffins? I checked the ingredients. We had them all, even the sun-dried tomatoes, which always reminded me of shrivelled-up ears, although they did give a rather special flavour.

Oh no, I was beginning to sound like Vera. Suddenly I realised I didn't want to make wanky Vera food. Forget foccacia, sun-dried things, balsamic vinegar, home-made pasta, goat's cheese, all that bullshitty stuff. Sandwiches, that's what I'd make, ordinary ones with thin white bread and ham and mustard. Cut off the crusts and garnish with parsley. It would be my campaign. A return to good plain food. Date scones! Vegemite on toast! Yes! This was only the beginning.

Next I lay on my bed and had a bit of a snooze. As I drifted off I remembered the love spell, safely hidden in the pocket of my dressing gown. Money in one pocket, magic spell in the other; a dressing gown of great riches and supernatural power.

The thing was, today was Friday, so if I was going to do the spell, tonight was the best night to harness the power of Venus, Planet of Romance. We had white candles in the laundry cupboard. Vera always kept a box in case of power failures. We didn't have a rose bush, though. Perhaps dried rose petals would be just as good . . . there were some dusty ones in the potpourri jar in the bathroom . . . but maybe it would wreck the spell if you didn't have proper rose petals . . . oh sleepy sleepy . . .

I was deep in a dream set in Las Vegas. I looked wildly fantastic: blue satin dress, blue satin high-heels, very big hair. I was about to win a million dollars. 'Bec is the winner,' the oily-smooth croupier announced. 'Bec, *Bec*', oh help, I wasn't in Las Vegas, I was in my bedroom and Mrs D was calling me because I was wanted on the phone. It was Nick. He was bringing some cool-sounding tunes to the party, bands like Foo Fighters and Magic Dirt. We talked for ages about music, until Mrs D called me for dinner.

'I gotta go, see ya tomorrow,' I said.

'Looking forward to it,' came the reply.

I could have been eating fried shoe for all the notice I took of dinner. I was spinning out. It didn't mean he liked me, though. I mean, of course he liked me, but there was liking and *liking*, wasn't there? Nah, think positive. The phone call was fate, a sign to complete the magic, do the spell, make him love me. I unearthed the candles, took them out of the packet, put three back in, held seven in my hand, savouring their cool waxy smoothness.

My stomach was tight, all anxious and twitchy. I suddenly knew I couldn't do the love spell. Was I afraid of magic? No, it wasn't that. It was Steve. He was goofy and lived in a daggy suburb and he wasn't an elegant dude like Nick was, but he was the reason I couldn't do the spell. I had to admit it. I liked them both.

What a mess. They were best friends, for a start. Had they talked about me to each other or not? Maybe between them they thought they had the whole thing sussed . . . but perhaps they hadn't talked at all. Perhaps each of them thought the other one was in with a chance? Or what if they both thought of me as just a girl, Jaz's friend Bec, no one special? That was another thing, what about Jaz? She'd hate me if she thought I was messing with her brother's head, letting him think I liked him, when I liked someone else as well. I knew I should have stayed away from the boy thing. And I should never, *never* have said yes to the stupid party. Mrs D stuck her head around the laundry door.

'What are you doing, Bec, all alone in the dark. Is everything okay?'

'Not really . . .'

'What's up?'

I burst into tears.

'Hey, it's all right, sweetie. Come on, into the lounge, come and talk.'

In between blowing my nose and sobbing, I blurted the whole thing out. It was a relief to tell someone. Ever since the night Jaz and I ended up at Steve's place I'd been feeling more and more confused. Mixed feelings. New feelings. Feelings I didn't know what to do with. I had pushed them all under, tried to ignore them, but now they all came bubbling out.

'What am I going to do? It's a total nightmare. I never want to see either of them ever again. I don't want to have the party, and anyhow I don't have anything to wear . . .'
I blew my nose hard and grinned, somewhat shakily. Letting it out was a relief but I felt a doofus as well.

'Whoa, hang on there . . . who said you can't like both of them? It sounds to me as if they both like you. You remind me of me when I was young and frisky, always in a hurry to get to the end of the story, never content to just lighten up and enjoy the ride. You're only fifteen, it's not like you have to marry either of them, you know. The party will be fun: all your friends, music, dancing . . . At the risk of sounding hippie-trippy, how about surrendering to the great mystery? Let go and trust things will work out just the way they're supposed to.'

'It's just . . .'

'Just what?'

'The sex thing.'

Mrs D raised her eyebrows in an uncertain but go-on sort of way. If I felt like a doofus before I felt like a double doofus now, but I might as well say it.

'If a guy is your friend, that's okay, but once you start kissing and everything, they want more, and then you're meant to be their girlfriend, or maybe they just dump you . . .' I tapered off.

'Well, boys certainly are horny creatures at that age, ain't that the truth. The decision is up to you, though, surely? You own your feelings and your body. You've got the power to say yes or no or maybe, once you figure out what feels right for you.'

'That's the problem, liking them both, when they're best friends . . .'

'Well, may the best man win. Or just keep them both as friends perhaps. Why not just enjoy the party and see what happens. But what's this about nothing to wear?'

I told Mrs D the saga of the dress, or rather my lack of a dress.

'I don't have anything special, and I don't want to wear any of Vera's stuff . . .'

'Mmm, I've got an idea. Mr Patrick is going over to my place in the morning to water my plants, he's going to pick up a few things for me. Why don't you just leave it with me . . .'

My heart didn't exactly leap at her words. I couldn't see my-self in one of Mrs D's baggy florals. Grown-ups have dodgy taste at the best of times.

That night I tossed and turned in my bed, trying to have faith in things turning out okay.

That was the thing about adults telling you stuff. It didn't matter how good the advice was, in the end you had to figure it out for yourself. At school I'd learned all the technical stuff. I could put a condom on a carrot, I knew the names of everything from a testicle to an ovary. Then there was the mother-daughter rave from Vera. 'Sex is a normal part of a loving, committed relationship,' Vera had said, trying to sound cool even though I know she was embarrassed. All very well for her to say that, but her values didn't quite match the reality of life in this century. Take Katherine and Kenzo, or Lisa and her love-life, for example. Like, what if you just wanted to try it with someone, get it over with, not be a virgin any more? Was that such a crime? I didn't think so, but it hadn't seemed to leave Katherine feeling very good. She wouldn't even talk about it.

I liked what Mrs D suggested. Enjoy the mystery, take your time, do what feels right to you. Which was all very well, but what *did* feel right to me?

pppppparty

Saturday passed in a blur. Josh and Bing helped me tidy the house. We put tea-lights everywhere, and set the table with a batik cloth and the big white candle in the wrought-iron holder that Vera used at dinner parties. Mrs D gave instructions from the comfort of her sofa.

'Bung the juice in the fridge. There's a packet of salted mixed nuts in the pantry, and serviettes if you want them. How about filling the ice trays?'

After lunch Megan and Mrs Murphy came to pick Bing up.

'Have a good one, Bec.' Bing gave me one of her extra-special tough little hugs. 'Save me some party food if ya can, okay? And don't let anyone mess with Begonia.'

Once Bing had gone the house went quiet. Josh was surfing the net, Mrs D put on some classical music and promptly dozed off. I hit the kitchen and did my thing with the sandwiches, covering them with a damp cloth to keep them moist, like my nana used to. I took the horrible school photo of me off the fridge door, and hid it under a pile of junk mail. School photos make you look your most dorky, and parents will insist upon displaying them, but there was no way I wanted my friends to see that particularly cheesy number.

I washed my hair and sat in the sun while it dried. It was a pity the courtyard was so crappy but I didn't really see the weeds and the broken pavers any more. I saw the dream garden, the garden to be.

I painted my toenails the colour of milky coffee. The same colour as Nick's arms, I remembered, and my tummy suddenly felt all queasy. My mind flooded with thoughts of the skate day at God Park. I remembered Nick and Steve whizzing around; princes of the air. I remembered how neat the night had been when Steve came over. He wasn't Mister Smooth like Nick but he was funny and nice and sort of comfortable. Like an older brother. Except that older brothers didn't try and pash you up. Now my stomach was really fluttery.

Think about something else. Clothes. I'd pretend to be really appreciative of the dorky dress but when Mrs D left I'd put on my jeans, Vera's green top and my green glass necklace. It wasn't the new and glamorous outfit I'd dreamed of but at least I wouldn't be Nice-Bec-in-Nice-Pink. The afternoon drifted by.

At six o'clock Mr Patrick arrived. It was obvious he'd made special efforts because his hair was slicked down and he was wearing a polo shirt. I wondered if he'd spent the afternoon doing a housework blitz as well because his cottage tended to be a bit, shall we say, disorganised. He handed me a bunch of flowers fresh from his garden, creamy chrysanthemums and ladder fern, all tied up in a flourish of brown paper.

'Yummy, thank you, they'll look great in the middle of the table.'

Mr P grinned like a happy Buddha.

'Did you get the stuff from my place?' Mrs D asked anxiously.

'Oh, that's right, it's in the boot, I hope I got the right thing. I'm not very up on women's clothing to be honest.'

This was going to be embarrassing. I didn't want to hurt Mrs D's feelings. I would have to do a good job of acting pleased.

~~~

'Sit on the couch and close your eyes, Bec.'

There was something in my hands, something satiny, something textured. I opened my eyes. It was the loveliest jacket I had ever seen. Creamy white satin, every inch covered in Chinese embroidery, roses, leaves, birds.

'It's for you. Try it on. I wore it with a black skirt, but maybe jeans . . .'

If the jacket had been made for me by angels it could not have fitted better. I hugged Mrs D tightly, trying not to cry. Not sad tears. Happy tears. Magic Chinese princess tears.

'Have fun, see you at midnight,' said Mrs D, and they were gone.

That was the difference between her and my mother. Vera would have been giving me heaps of instructions. 'Don't get anything on the carpet, don't use the good plates, there won't be any alcohol, will there?' I could hear her voice lurking in the hallway. My well-meaning, controlling mother.

It was too early to get dressed. I tried to read the *Face*

magazine that Jaz had lent me, but I couldn't concentrate. I kept hopping up to shift a cushion from one spot to another, then shifting it back again. For goodness' sake, they're your friends, not the Interior Design Police, I told myself. Whose dumb idea was it to have a party anyway? God, I'm going to kill Lisa. I turned on the telly. Judge Judy was lecturing a woman who'd stolen her sister's husband. It's such a dumb program. I can't imagine why anyone would choose to be humiliated like that in front of millions of viewers. Maybe they got paid heaps. Maybe they were actors, or maybe they were just total idiots. Anyhow it helped me pass the next half hour. At times like these television is the perfect drug: mind-numbing, legal, easily obtained.

Six-thirty. How was I going to survive a whole hour and a half of this nerve-wracking combination of excitement and terror? I put on my Ani di Franco tape and turned it up to the max, which helped quite a bit, and went up to my bedroom. With the bed made and the desk tidied it looked okay. Not that anyone was going to see my bedroom, were they?

Next, a shower. I lathered myself with dewberry soap, sprayed on Vera's Issey Missayake perfume, used heaps of her expensive body goo products. Tried to put my hair up. Made four attempts but finally gave up and left it down. I put on my jeans, my wonderful jacket, and my black sandals. Twirled around in front of the mirror. I looked great.

At ten to eight Julia and Katherine arrived. Katherine was

kind of nervous and went round squawking about everything. Julia headed straight for the bathroom to re-do her make-up. I put the salmon dip, the Ritz crackers and the yummy chocolate cake on the table. I lit the tea-lights, and the chunky white candle. Katherine lit the rose-patchouli incense. Everything was ready, all we needed was more people.

'Hey,' said Julia, emerging from the bathroom. 'Let's get into this. I chilled it in the freezer without my mother noticing.' She waved the bottle of champagne in the air.

'Don't shake it around, it'll fizz up,' Katherine pointed out.

I untwisted the heavy silvery wrapping, popped the cork, and poured three glasses.

~~~~

Parties are bizarre. One minute you're all alone and waiting, certain that no one will come, worrying that you look a dag or that it will turn out a flop. The scene is set but the cast is missing. Then, suddenly, it's all happening, party-a-go-go, and you don't get to catch your breath until hours later. That's what my party was like, anyhow.

No sooner had we opened the champagne than Lisa, Tom and Jeremy arrived. Lisa looked totally classy in tight black bell-bottoms and a tight black t-shirt. Her blond hair was all messed up and moussed up. She had on sparkly fake diamond earrings, and very red lipstick.

'Here, darling, some sweeties,' she said in a weird European accent, handing me a platter piled high with liquorice allsorts, chocolates, jelly babies, Smarties, toffees in turquoise and pink shiny papers. Jeremy was clutching two tall brown bottles of beer and wearing the loudest Mambo shirt I'd ever seen. It was bright blue and patterned with red islands and Polynesian dancing girls and dolphins and clouds and canoes and bones and other lurid stuff. Tom was rather quiet, although I think in comparison to Jeremy and Lisa anyone would have seemed quiet. He headed straight for the CD player and put on a CD that he produced from a Sony PlayStation DiscHolder.

'That sounds great, who is it?' Katherine asked shyly. 'Jamiroquai, Save the World. This track is called *Shut up and Dance*,' said Tom.

'Good plan. Give me a beer,' said Lisa. She swivelled her hips and started to boogie, and we all joined in.

Around quarter to nine, just when I was starting to panic in a fuzzy champagney sort of way, Jaz and Nick and Sam and Steve rocked up.

'Sorry we're late. We couldn't find Pete,' Jaz explained. 'We went to his father's place in Leederville. He said he'd be there but there was no one home, no note, nothing.' She handed me the sushi and Sam put a six-pack of Cooper's Pale Ale on the table. He was even more handsome than I remembered from the record shop. Dark curly hair, olive skin, and those intelligent eyes.

'Hey, Bec,' said Steve, grinning. His fish tattoo stood out like a lucky totem on his muscular arm.

Nick was the last one to come in. He didn't say anything, just beamed and came and stood beside me. Jaz poured herself a beer. Steve bit into a piece of sushi. Now my party could really begin.

weird threads

I wish I could say that my party was the best night of my life but it wasn't. First, there was the Turkish Carpet Incident. You couldn't say we followed the blue on this one, or drifted on yellow or floated smoothly along on apricot. This is one of the twisted bits.

Things were going great. The food was fine, especially the chocolate cake. We polished off the champagne and the beer but no one got stupid. We were having a really good time. We danced. Sometimes we all danced together, sometimes we danced in pairs. Jeremy and Steve were the funniest, with their very own invention: The Dinosaur Thump. Jaz made up a dance as well: The Imaginary Tango. Her beaded sandals invented happy, mad rhythms as Sam whirled her around like a Mambo King. They were great together, so happy and alive. I danced with Nick and with Steve and with Tom. I was taking Mrs D's advice, just having fun.

It must have been about ten o'clock when I noticed that Nick and Tom and Jeremy were missing. They weren't hanging out and dancing with the rest of us. When I went into the kitchen to get more ice for the orange juice they weren't in there, either. I checked the patio. Maybe Nick was telling them the plan for the garden, but no, they weren't outside. It was strange, but there wasn't much I could do about it so I went back and danced with the others. Katherine finally got up the courage to put on Greatest Hits of the Seventies and we all got right into it. Jaz was swaying around the room like an elegant lunatic when we heard Jeremy thundering down the stairs, Nick and Tom following close behind, making a huge commotion. They all looked utterly panic stricken.

'Bec, where's the water main?' Nick yelled. 'Quick, where's the water main? We have to turn it off.'

Imagine ten completely bamboozled party people racing around outside in the darkness looking for a water main. I had absolutely no idea where it was. It was one of those things only my father knew, in case he needed to turn it off to fix a tap washer or something. I didn't even know why I was looking for it, exactly, although I did hear the words 'flooded the carpet' and 'smashed basin', so I knew things were pretty serious. Imagine ten minutes of total chaos and screaming and yelling and falling over in the dark. Just in case you ever need to know, the water main at 127 Mahogany Avenue, Parkerville, Perth, Western Australia is located near the front of the property, to the left of the letterbox, beside a red geranium bush, underneath a whole lot of ivy.

After we'd turned off the water and done what we could

to mop up the flood with towels and stuff, we all flopped down on the carpet in the lounge.

'So, what happened, cowboys?' asked Lisa in her I-am-so-cool drawl. 'Come on, dudes, out with it.'

Tom looked at Nick. Nick looked at Jeremy. Jeremy looked at Tom. Silence. All three faces had the same expression, a mixture of goofy embarrassment and half-arsed pride. Jeremy blurted out, 'Don't look at me, man, you are the one that . . .'

'Okay, right, well, um, we went up to have a bit of a smoke—' began Nick.

'And Nick sat on the handbasin,' Tom joined in.

'And the bloody thing broke,' Jeremy added, and the three of them burst out laughing.

There was a shocked silence while the rest of us absorbed the information.

'God, sorry, Bec,' Nick contributed, trying to be sensible. I giggled. It *was* pretty funny, although telling my parents about it might not be so hilarious.

'It's cool,' I said, 'or should I make that "It's wet".'

Things went quiet after that. Steve put on a neat CD called *Nightmares on Wax*, really mellow music. Julia and Jaz and Sam started dancing again, not raging, just sort of gently grooving around. Jeremy flaked out on the sofa and called someone on his mobile. Tom buried his head in one of Lewis's photography books.

Katherine and I went into the kitchen to make coffee. I was

half watching Steve, standing over by the window all by himself, as I poured boiling water into the cups.

Damn. That's what happens when you aren't paying attention. I'd splashed it all over the bench, and oh no, now there was a tiny coffee stain on the sleeve of my beautiful jacket. I took the stairs two at a time, trying to remember what you're supposed to do to remove coffee stains. Vera has a remedy for every emergency but all I could think of was, 'don't use hot water, it sets the stain'.

I stood in the bathroom, dabbing my sleeve with a soapy flannel, trying not to get it too wet. Whew, it came out okay. I gave my hair a quick brush and was spraying on a bit more Issey when I heard giggling, muffled voices.

No need to go down the hall and look. I knew who it was. Lisa and Nick. In my bedroom.

I stood there for the busiest sixty seconds of my entire life. First I felt numb. Then I felt angry. For one crazy second I contemplated opening my bedroom door and yelling, 'How dare you!' Then I felt sad, then I felt embarrassed. Then I had a flash of I-knew-this-would-happen. Then I felt pissed off again, and then I just felt hurt and tired. I stood there for a moment longer, my heart pounding like some kind of wounded creature.

Then I went downstairs and pretended that nothing had happened.

The worst thing was, they didn't come out for about a million years.

After a while Jeremy asked sleepily, 'Hey, man, where are Nick and Lisa?'

No one replied, and suddenly it dawned on him. His face turned the same colour as his Mambo shirt. By then everyone else had guessed what was happening. Jaz was the only one to put her thoughts into words. She came and put her arm round me.

'My brother is one dumb shmuck,' she whispered. The others bustled around doing the dishes and tidying up.

Steve and I sat on the back step. 'Nick is just Nick,' he said gently. 'He's kind of unpredictable.'

'Yeah,' I said. 'Well, I hate him anyway. Not to mention Lisa.'

'Yeah. But hey,' Steve continued, 'look, Bec, it's a new constellation, The Wonky Banana.'

'What about that one over there?' I answered. 'The Dagger . . . The Dagger of the Evil Friend.'

Steve put his arm round me. I leant against him and bawled my eyes out.

~~~

Midnight came and everyone went home.

~~~

I sat alone on the step, under the big night of stars. So wide, so dark, so vast.

I still felt tragic, but somehow my smallness in the bigness of space made me feel better.

Somewhere somebody lay dying, saying goodbye to it all.

Somewhere a funny little baby was being born. On the other side of the world a girl like me was wondering what to wear to school, and her brother was putting heaps of butter on two bits of brown toast.

Eggleton came and sat beside me. 'I've been betrayed, you know,' I said, and giggled. 'Love hurts,' I told him. No response, or maybe he did purr a little more sympathetically than usual. 'Bugger it, cat,' I said, 'I'm going to bed.' And I did.

postscript

bing

The sea monkeys were a great disappointment to me but I don't care. I am going to use the fact that they were so pathetic to make Vera feel guilty so she will let me have a dog. A greyhound would be really good or a cocker spaniel. When I grow up I am not going to go stupid like Bec and get all thingy about boys.

josh

There are birds called snow geese that can fly a thousand kilometres without stopping. This world is an amazing place and I am a boy who lives in it.

damages

Carpet Bill: One Turkish hall runner.

Special treatment: dry and treat for mildew. $147.00

Plumbing Repairs: One case of beer and a big thanks to Mr Patrick.

lisa

None of my friends are talking to me but I don't care. It's not my fault if Nick liked me more than he liked Bec. I'm going to leave school and head south to the forest. I want to save the trees. I want to save myself. I will get a jewel in my nose, a garnet or an emerald. I will live in a tent and fall in love with a man with dirty feet and poetry in his soul. He won't be easily led, not some silly boy, who bonks you and then forgets to call. My forest man will have an interesting name like Jarrah, or Reuben. He's waiting for me somewhere, I know he is. We will never live in the suburbs, where they cut down all the trees and name streets after them. One day we'll have a baby. She will be the most beautiful baby in the world and we will name her Sunshine Ruby.

pete

My father kicked me out. Without any warning. He came downstairs, made himself a cup of coffee, sat down at the kitchen table, rolled himself a cigarette. It could have been any day, a same-old, same-old day, but it wasn't. It was a Saturday afternoon and I was supposed to be going to a party with my friends that night. He didn't even look me in the eye. 'I've had it with you. Go and live at your mother's,' he said. 'You need to get a job, get your act together.' Just like that, man. Just like that. So I'm back living with my mother, for now, anyway. I got myself a job doing the night-shift in a bakery. It's not so bad.

julia

I want a handbag embroidered with roses. I want tortoise-shell sunglasses. I want to live in New York. I want to go clubbing and dance the night away in bare feet. I want to look absolutely gorgeous and always wear sexy red lipstick, even when I'm old. I want to eat bagels for breakfast on Fifth Avenue with a handsome Mexican boy. I want to design clothes soft enough for angels, sexy enough for urban cow-girls. I want excessive amounts of nice stuff. I want to be incredibly famous. I want to fly first class to Paris. I will do it. I absolutely will.

katherine

I wish I was thinner. I wish there were no such things as zits, homework, or exams. I wish my mother didn't yell at me when she was angry, and that she believed in giving me large amounts of pocket money. I wish Julia liked me better than she liked anyone else. I wish my legs were thin and muscular. I wish my hair was not so red and wild. I wish I was as crea-tive as Bec and as funky as Jaz. I wish I could do cartwheels. I wish I could sing like Macey Gray. I wish Tom would like me.

jaz

What I want. I want to get to know Sam better, because he's so cool and he bothers to think for himself. I want to live somewhere brilliant like London or Prague. I want to mix with poets and artists and musicians and circus people. I want to get into the music scene. I want to do things that challenge me. I want to learn to fly, be a DJ, do a kickflip, be an acrobat. I don't want to ever just stay the same. I want my parents to grow up and stop acting dumb, like going for the fast easy dollar, and drinking too much. They've almost forgotten how to be kind. I want them to be happy, but even if they can't I'm not going to let it cripple me. I am a white frangipani blossom that smells like heaven. I am the one and only Jaz.

nick

Things are pretty desperate for me lately. I broke three skateboard decks in two weeks, and my Uni work fell in a heap because my garden project got canned at the last minute. I'm doing a garden for a girl called Bec instead. Me and my mates are laying the bricks next Saturday. Bec is going to make a mosaic in the middle from blue and green and purple tiles. I stuffed up totally with Bec, though. I sort of liked her, and she liked me, too, but I got way too ripped at her party. My friends and I managed to destroy a handbasin and a carpet, and I ended up shagging one of her friends, this blond girl called Lisa. We were pretty out of it. We were dancing, then we were kissing, and the rest just sort of happened. Jaz is furious with me. Lisa doesn't particularly want to see me again, and I think Bec is only still talking to me because of the garden thing. Jaz says I am a total fuckwit. Right now I agree with her somewhat.

eloise

Soon we're going home to Perth. I'm kind of glad. Living in New York is pretty cool but it can get a little crazy and I miss my friends, especially Bec. She wrote to me how she met some hell-fun guys who skate, so that should be a blast. I can't wait to swim at Cottlesloe beach and drink a mocha at Tropicana. One thing that is really foul in America is the coffee. It comes in these huge polystyrene containers and tastes like old shoe.

jeremy

I really like Lisa but I don't have a chance with her. She shagged someone else at a party, which pretty much says it all. Lisa is one of those girls that want something, something I can't even describe properly. I just know that I don't seem to have it. What do I have? Well, I have feet that smell pretty foul. I'm on to it, though. I just bought some Odour Eaters and every night I wash my feet with my mum's Peppermint Foot Lotion, although I wouldn't tell anyone that if you paid me. Apart from that, my physical attributes are okay. I am medium height, medium build and have brown hair. My penis is a pretty good size. I measured it, after reading an article in *Playboy*. I seem to be above average, so that's good. It's a pity I never get a chance to try it out though, which is another thing I don't exactly spread around town. I do have a car, though, which is a real asset for a guy, and I own some very cool Mambo shirts. One day I'll find a girl who likes me just the way I am. Hopefully. Meanwhile I have to concentrate on my Uni study and not drink so much beer on the weekends. I should probably stay away from party drugs, too. I can do that. Hopefully.

tom

I met a girl at a party. I like her a lot. Her name's Katherine. She has big wild red hair and a big wide smile. She also has heaps of freckles. My uncle has freckles, too, but on him they look like a sprinkling of red dirt. On Katherine they look pretty. At the party I was too shy to ask her to dance. I asked my friend if I should ask her out and he says I should definitely go for it. Therefore I will. I really hope Katherine says yes. There are heaps of girls around who are really snobby or silly, but there is something really special about Katherine.

steve

I am the happiest guy on Planet Perth.

sam

Adults always ask you what you want to do when you grow up. I think it's a completely stupid question. Why do we have to choose one thing? Why can't we do heaps of things? I never want to wear a suit and a tie and go to work in an airless office, spending my days pushing meaningless bits of paper around and saying yes to the boss. If that's growing up then I don't want to ever grow up. I just want to live my life and be happy. I want to play my guitar and listen to my music. I want to take every day as it comes. I want to go to America with Jaz and drive down Route 66 in a metallic blue Buick. I want to see Ireland and Mexico and travel around South America wearing a black hat like Tom Waits. As that old guitar player in The Who said, 'I hope I die before I get old.'

bec

I'm going to buy myself a new journal. A big one with fresh white pages. I'm going to write down my secrets, and learn to draw. I'm going to fill the pages with pictures of things that I love. I'm going to put the rest of my money in the bank so I can go travelling when I leave school, but first I'm going to buy myself a kimono, a blue silk one.

Vera and Lewis have been home for three days. Vera is still talking a mile a minute, showing us things, finding little goodies as she unpacks. When I told my mother about Steve, she sort of panicked.

'I don't think you should get too involved with boys. Not yet, darling,' she said, looking anxious.

'Mum,' I said, 'Steve is a honey.' Which he is. He's the best.

Maybe he's not Mr Cool but he isn't Mr Unpredictable either. He's goofy, friendly and funny, and I really, really like him. My parents have only met him once. He and Lewis got on great. I'm hoping Vera will chill a bit when she gets used to the idea that I have a boyfriend.

Mothers only know a certain amount about their children. Sometimes they get too worried about stuff. They get all burdened with fear. At least Vera knows she's doing it.

'I worry about you, Bec,' she says. 'I worry that you will do all the crazy stuff I did when I was your age, but that you won't be as lucky as I was.'

'Mum, get a grip, I'm not going to get pregnant or turn out a heroin addict,' I say, and I give her a hug. 'Save all your worrying for Bing, you're going to need it,' I remind her. Vera rolls her eyeballs and smiles, then she goes back to inventing something delicious using prunes, kirsch and marscapone for the new book. *Desserts to Die For*, it's called.

It's so good to have my father home again, back from travelling, back from the dark. We sit on the back step together and he tells me about the Pueblo Indian village site in Taos.

'You can still see the black smudges in the caves, from the cooking fires, Bec,' he says. 'You can walk along trails that Indian feet walked on hundreds of years ago. You can feel the ghosts of the women and the children, the men, and the prairie dogs,' he tells me. 'We'll go there one day, Bec, you and me and Mum and Josh and Bing.'

'I'd like that,' I say.

Lewis goes inside and I sit by myself for a while longer.

The sky is full of bright new stars, just waiting for me to name them.

~~~

In my bedroom the tiny peep-show people are dancing in the dark.